ANTHROPOLOGY AND THE WESTERN TRADITION

Toward an Authentic Anthropology

Jacob Pandian
California State University, Fullerton

WAVELAND

PRESS, INC.

Prospect Heights, Illino

D1446815

For information about this book, write or call:

Waveland Press, Inc.
P.O. Box 400
Prospect Heights, Illinois 60070
(312) 634-0081

Copyright © 1985 by Waveland Press, Inc.

ISBN 0-88133-127-9

All rights reserved. No part of this book may be reproduced, stored in a retrieval system, or transmitted in any form or by any means without permission in writing from the publisher.

Printed in the United States of America

9 8 7 6 5 4

Contents

Preface vii

Chapter 1   Introduction: Objectives and Scope of this Study 1

Objectives   1
The Quest for Human Integration   5
The Range of Human Possibilities and
    the Judeo-Christian Orientation   7
Toward an Authentic Anthropology   12

Part I: Inventing Human Nature

Chapter 2   The Teaching of Anthropology 17

The Anthropology Curriculum in
    American Academia   17
Anthropology as a Holistic Study of Humankind   21
The Empirical Study of Cultural and
    Human Variation   24
Continuity and Change   26

Chapter 3   Culture, Symbol and Myth 28

The Development of Theoretical Formulations About
    Culture in the Western Tradition   28
The Debates and Controversies Concerning the
    Conceptualization of Culture   32
Symbol and Myth   36

**Chapter 4   The Construction of the Self and the
                  Formulation of Ethnic Identity** 41

The Mythology of the Self   41

The Mythology of the Ethnic Self   43
Acculturation   45

Part II: Inventing the Human Other

**Chapter 5   The Mythology of the Abnormal Human Other
in the Western Tradition** 49

The Judeo-Christian Dichotomy of the Self   49
The Fascination with the Abnormal   52

**Chapter 6   The Mythology of the Fossil Human Other
in the Western Tradition** 55

The Fossil Other in the Judeo-Christian Lineal
Conception of History   55
The Fossil Other in the Late Renaissance and the
Enlightenment   56
The Fossil Other in the 19th Century   57
Exteriorization and Interiorization of the Other   60

**Chapter 7   The Mythology of the Savage Other in the
Western Tradition** 62

The Locus of the Symbol of the Savage Other   62
Land and Order: The Discovery of the New World   64
The Symbol of the Savage Other:
Differences Between Renaissance and the
Enlightenment Anthropology   67

**Chapter 8   The Mythology of the Black Other in the
Western Tradition** 70

Classifications of Humans Based on Color During the
Renaissance and the Enlightenment   70
The Origin of the Concept of Race   76
The Invention of the Black Other   79

**Chapter 9   The Mythology of the Ethnographic Other in the
Western Tradition** 85

The Invention of the Ethnographic Other   85
Renaissance Beginnings of the Ethnographic
Tradition   86
Participant Observation and Objectivity   87
Data on the Ethnographic Other as Capital   90
Interpretive Data and Allegorical Data   92

Part III: Inventing Anthropology

Chapter 10   The Anthropology of Anthropology 98

Anthropology in Culture   98
The Cultural Constitution of Modern
    Anthropology in the Western Tradition   99
The Study of the History of Anthropology as a
    Sub-Discipline of Anthropology   107

Chapter 11   Anthropology in the Humanities 110

Interpretation of the Human Other   110
Science and the Humanities   111
Science and the Sociopolitical Context   113
Anthropology, History and the Anthropology
    of History   115
The Need to Teach an Introductory Course in
    Anthropology as Part of the Humanities   118

Chapter 12   Toward an Authentic Anthropology 121

Bibliography 127

Preface

In this book I present an interpretation of anthropology, its intellectual and social foundations, its structure and meaning. I have focused on the question of why it is considered necessary and valid to study other peoples in order to understand ourselves and the nature of humankind. I suggest that this question may be answered by investigating the epistemes and paradigms — understood loosely as the prevailing cultural structures of meaning — of the Western tradition. This requires the analysis of symbols that embody and signify the nature of humankind and the human self, that provide the foundation for relating ourselves to other peoples. I believe that such an analysis may shed some light on the strengths as well as the weaknesses of anthropology.

I am grateful to my wife, Sue Parman, who has given me immense support, and my daughter, Gigi, who has given me immense hope, for their gifts of love and understanding. I dedicate this book to them with love and gratitude, and to the poets of the Tamil bardic tradition of about 2,000 years ago who proclaimed, *Yathum Urae, Yavarum Kaeleer* ("I belong to every country, let everyone hear").

J. Pandian
California State University,
Fullerton
June, 1984

Chapter 1

Introduction

Objectives and Scope of this Study

Objectives

Of all the disciplines concerned with the study of humankind, anthropology, as the explicitly universalistic study of humanity, has the potential to promote humanistic discourse that can bring peoples of the world closer to each other and encourage an appreciation, respect and sympathy for cultural differences. At the same time, however, anthropology has often been invoked to claim the natural superiority or inferiority of certain peoples; and the "scientific" theories of anthropology have reflected and supported the biases and preconceptions of the periods in which they were developed (for example, see Gould 1981).

One objective in writing this book is to provide the beginning student in anthropology with an understanding of how anthropology fits in the social and intellectual tradition of the West. Such an inquiry requires an analysis of how anthropological data are used, and have in the past been used in the Western tradition. Why are anthropological studies accepted as valid in the West? Upon what features of Western civilization are the assumptions about non-Western peoples based? Can we relate the shifts in concern with certain types of anthropological data (for example, skull shapes in the 19th century and frequency of rape in the 20th) to the needs of the West itself rather than to some rational process of discovery?

My goal is not to debunk anthropology but to encourage an understanding of why certain kinds of interpretations and explanations of other peoples became important at certain times in the Western tradition. By showing how anthropological concerns are linked with cultural concerns of the West and how anthropology has a societal function in the West, I hope to contribute to the discipline's realization of its potential to promote humanistic discourse about diverse peoples and cultures.

A second objective of this book is to introduce the beginning student to

1

the fact that the nature of anthropological theories cannot be grasped without understanding the contexts and meanings of the relationship between the West and non-Western peoples. After the 16th century Western images of the non-West and of humankind in general contained in anthropological theories reflected certain types of dominant-subordinate relationships between the West and the non-West. Historically, these images were often used to justify the displacement or elimination of non-Western peoples from their own land, colonizing or exploiting them economically, and enslaving or using them for labor. To understand the contexts and meanings of the relationships between the West and the non-West and their implications for the development and maintenance of anthropology, the beginning student of anthropology must have some familiarity with global history beginning about 1500 A.D. when the West began to assert its political-economic dominance and Western scholars began to use the data on non-Western peoples in their discourse on human nature, mind, self, etc., in order to assert the intellectual and moral superiority of the West. The anthropologist Eric Wolf has made a significant contribution in this area of knowledge, most notably in his recent book titled *Europe and the People Without History* (1982) in which he shows how the Western search for economic resources outside Europe after the 15th century generated certain types of production and distribution processes in which the non-West became linked in the shaping of Western economic, political and intellectual history. Also, new types of economic, political and intellectual constellations evolved in the non-Western world, either imposed by the West or created in response to the nature of economic and political relationships between the West and the non-West.

A third objective in writing this book is to offer an interpretation of Western cultural structures that have produced the disciplinary orientation of anthropology. I suggest that there is an important link between the Judeo-Christian orientation and modern anthropology. I discuss briefly the assumptions about the nature of self and the nature of knowledge, and offer my interpretations in the framework of cultural or "symbolic" analysis.

I have organized the different interpretations offered in this book into three parts, flanked by an introduction (Chapter 1) and a conclusion (Chapter 12). Part I is called "Inventing Human Nature," Part II "Inventing the Human Other," and Part III "Inventing Anthropology." Each part is preceded by an introductory statement which explains these titles. A brief description of the three parts is offered below.

Part I, "Inventing Human Nature," which includes Chapters Two, Three, and Four, provides an analysis of contemporary anthropology, with specific reference to the conceptualization of culture, symbol, myth, self, acculturation and ethnicity. The concepts discussed in Part I are used to interpret the Western tradition in Part II.

In Part II, "Inventing the Human Other," composed of Chapters Five through Nine, I use the concepts of contemporary anthropology described in Part I to understand the Western tradition, and examine how and why various images of non-Western human others have been promoted by anthropology. In Chapters Five and Six, I analyze the cultural logic embodied in the mythology of the abnormal other and the fossil other in the Western tradition. Chapter Seven examines the mythology of the savage other, or the anthropological descriptions and explanations of Native Americans who were the primary referent for the conceptualization of savage, irrational humanity. Chapter Eight examines the mythology of the black other, or the anthropological descriptions and explanations of sub-Saharan Africans, who became the primary empirical referent for the conceptualization of racially inferior humanity. Chapter Nine analyzes the mythology of the ethnographic other, or the timelessness of those who are studied by contemporary anthropologists.

Part III, "Inventing Anthropology," composed of Chapters Ten and Eleven, examines the emergence of anthropology in the Western tradition. It offers an interpretation of anthropology as part of the humanities, and suggests a method by which anthropologists can study history as part of culture.

Although the view of modern anthropology as an aspect of the Western tradition is central to the interpretations offered in this book, it is beyond the scope of this book to undertake a major analysis of the Western tradition. The purpose of this study is to investigate how and why non-Western human beings were defined, signified and used for defining the nature of humanity in various ways since 1500 A.D. In other words, I am concerned with examining the discourse on humankind (in which data on non-Western peoples are used) that began after the 16th century within the Western tradition.

The terms "West" and "Western tradition" have been widely used, and with different referents. I delineate the West as that area which is geographically identified as Europe, and I also include European settlements in other parts of the world. The term "West" may be used synonymously with "the Western tradition." By Western tradition I mean the basic paradigms or epistemes (metaphors, cultural modes of validating knowledge, etc.) of intellectual discourse which may be distinguished from other traditions of discourse such as the Hindu tradition or the Chinese tradition that have historically evolved distinctive types of discourse concerning humanity. This book focuses on one aspect of the Western tradition, namely, the interpretations, explanations and evaluations of non-Western peoples.

The designation of "Western" geographical and intellectual boundaries is problematic and requires clarification. If we begin the discussion of the Western tradition with the Greeks, it is difficult to draw a line between what we regard now as the Middle East and Europe. Greek and Roman traditions covered large areas of the Middle East at different times; and Christianity, which made essential, fundamental contributions to the shaping of the Western tradition after the 5th century A.D., began in the Middle East. The Islamic tradition of the Middle East also had a great impact in parts of Europe, especially during the crusades of the 11th to 14th centuries. It is also necessary to remember that after the 4th century A.D., until the Byzantine Empire collapsed in the 15th century, Europe had a western and an eastern wing, the latter retaining more of the earlier Greco-Roman and Middle-Eastern cultural patterns.

From the 12th century on, the role of major contributor to the Western tradition passed from one region of Europe to another. For a few centuries, Italy was at the forefront in trade and intellectual activities. Italy's prominence was followed by that of Portugal and Spain, and by the 17th century, the sphere of economic/political dominance shifted to the countries of north-west Europe, primarily England, France, Holland and Denmark. As pointed out earlier, this book is concerned with investigating a certain type of discourse about humankind which became important after the 16th century. Although major economic, political, and commercial developments occurred during the four centuries preceding the 16th century, during which various regions of Europe made crucial contributions to the shaping of Western consciousness, after the 16th century, northwestern Europe began to function as the major economic and political power, and as a representation of what would be identified as significant intellectual discourse concerning humankind in non-theological terms.

Political/economic dominance in the modern world is to a large extent a function of the power which countries have as producers of goods (the producers of manufactured goods dominating the countries that provide raw materials), and the control they exert on the world financial market. In recent times, the United States has typified the dominance of the Western tradition. Thus, even though Latin America is part of "the West" by virtue of its historical connection to European settlement, it is not uncommon for many Latin Americans to identify the United States as the West. Most of what I discuss in this book under the category "Western tradition" deals with the paradigms and epistemes that were generated in north-western Europe or in those places, such as the United States, settled by north-western Europeans.

Throughout this book I refer to various "periods" in Western history. The periodization of the Western tradition is done for scholarly convenience, and scholars disagree as to the boundaries and character of the various periods. This book uses the following temporal delineation: The 5th to 15th centuries A.D. constitute the Middle Ages or Medieval Period. The first 600 years of this period are identified as the Dark Ages. Overlapping the Medieval Period is the Scholastic Period, from the 10th to 17th centuries A.D., of which the 14th to 17th centuries constitute the Renaissance. The

16th and 17th centuries are identified as the late Renaissance, and the 18th century as the Enlightenment.

The beginning student should not assume that these periods constitute sharply delineated cultural epochs. Historians focusing on the significance of particular periods in shaping the consciousness of the Western tradition find such delineations useful. They argue, for example, that cultural processes such as intense religious discourse on the nature of humankind and the universe occurred during the Scholastic Period, a humanistic revival of learning during the Renaissance, and the idealization of rationality during the Enlightenment. But it must be emphasized that multiple cultural processes occurred in the same period, and there is much more continuity between periods than is conveyed by the use of such concepts.

The Quest for Human Integration

People everywhere, at all times, have asked the question, "What is humankind?" This question is linked with the question, "Who am I?" or "What am I?" We identify these questions and their various answers as "theological," "folk," or "cultural" orientations, distinguishing the anthropological answer as naturalistic (because it locates humans in nature), culturalistic (because it views human behavioral reality as a humanly created cultural reality), and comparative (because it seeks to discover the differences and similarities in the cultural construction of reality).

Anthropological answers about the nature of humankind have profound significance or implications for the question, "Who am I?" or "What am I?" and for the conception of the self in general. As opposed to the theological or folk conception of the self with reference to the *internal* or traditional symbols of religion, language, nation, caste, tribe, etc., anthropological conceptions of the self have been made with reference to the *external* or anthropologically created symbols of other peoples, primarily non-Western peoples. Symbols such as Negro, Primitive, savage, cannibal, and specifically the symbols such as "magical other," "dreaming other," and "rape-free other" that are discussed in this book, became popular in the West.

Questions raised in this book include the following: Why did anthropological symbols become significant in the Western tradition? Why were these symbols used as vehicles to conceptualize the nature of humankind and the human self?

I suggest that it is necessary to examine the Judeo-Christian symbol(s) of divinity and the Christian conception of the human self in order to understand the role of the anthropological symbols of human others. Within the Judeo-Christian orientation (discussed in the following section of this chapter and in Chapter Five), the divine being is represented as the embodiment of perfection, which excludes many of the characteristics of the human condition. In the Christian orientation, human experiences of "weakness," "sexuality," "greed," etc. are viewed as alien to those who are linked with the Christian deity. The Christian conception of the self is created with a contrast between the true self, conceptualized with reference to the Christian deity, and the untrue self conceptualized with reference to Satan or the alien, evil characteristics of non-Christian peoples. The true self has the positive attributes of being truly human in the eyes of God, and the untrue self has the negative attributes of being a fallen person or sinner, a person without grace, a pagan.

Anthropological symbols, in the form of empirical referents, became important in popular as well as scholarly use after the 16th century: specific peoples represented cannibalism or satyrism; the West was represented as the embodiment of rationality, perfection, etc. (like the divine being) as opposed to non-Western peoples being represented as irrational and imperfect and as examples of behavior that were excluded from the true self and linked with the untrue self.

Beyond the above use of anthropological symbols (a use which continues today in the identification of non-Western peoples with exotic, sexual, religious customs), there also developed a theoretical body of knowledge that dealt with human integration.

Anthropological models of human integration convey the idea that despite the great differences in cultural forms, there are cultural universals; and that despite differences in physical appearances, there is a basic biological unity of humankind. Anthropology addresses the question, "What is humankind?", by identifying the factors that separate and unite humankind, and by incorporating them in different models of human integration.

Anthropology has sought to synthesize the true self (us) and the untrue self (the human other) in formulating theories concerning humankind as a whole. In other words, anthropology brings together the true self, which shares the attributes of what is accepted as valid within the Western tradition, and the untrue self of the human other, which has the characteristics which are alien to the Western tradition. Modern anthropology was born out of the need in the West to dichotomize and to reconcile the true self and the untrue self in comprehending the unity of mankind. I discuss the issues related to the conceptualization of the self in Chapter Four.

During the 18th century, the dominant model of integration identified the differences separating humanity in terms of rationality and irrationality, and located the "human us" in the category of rationality and the "human other" in the category of irrationality. This model later became a racial, hierarchical model which identified different racial mentalities which produced inferior or superior cultural forms. The racial mind producing superior cultural forms was that of the human us; the human other produced inferior cultural forms.

In contemporary anthropology, a dominant model of human integration dichotomizes the "conscious" and the "unconscious," and implies the existence of a conscious human us and an unconscious human other.

Who is defined as the human other, and how is the human other represented? At different times and in different places, depending on the needs of the particular Western society which is describing a specific human other, the images and attributes of the human other have varied. What specific peoples (American Indians? sub-Saharan Africans?) are used to represent otherness? Is the human other described as a savage? If so, is he a noble savage or debased savage? Is the human other described as belonging to a primeval, static, simple society? When and why did these shifts in image and use of the human other occur? Chapters Seven, Eight and Nine describe various anthropological symbols of human otherness (the savage other, the black other, and the ethnographic other).

The Range of Human Possibilities and the Judeo-Christian Orientation

In writing the history of anthropology, scholars locate the beginnings of anthropology in different historical periods depending on how they conceptualize the important distinguishing feature of anthropology.

Some trace the beginnings of anthropology to the non-theological views of man in Greco-Roman times (e.g., Malefijt 1976 and Honigmann 1976). However, naturalistic (i.e., non-theological) ideas about human nature and culture, and theories about progress or development of human institutions, existed in Greco-Roman as well as in other civilizations. I would argue that what makes anthropology distinctive is not its naturalistic worldview but its use of other groups to understand "us" and humanity.

The Greeks did not consider the study of non-Greeks a serious or significant mode of inquiry. They did not believe it necessary to study other peoples to understand themselves or the nature of humanity. From introspection and observation they derived concepts and theories to discuss the primordial man, the unity of mankind, biological and cultural evolution, and other concepts which are important concerns of modern anthropology. While the Greeks and Romans collected data on other peoples, they did not consider these data to contain hidden truths which must be examined to reveal the nature of humankind. Such data were thought interesting, a source of humor, perhaps, but were not charged with significance; they did not afford the Greeks access to truth about the nature of the self and Man.

Anthropology's uniqueness as a discipline stems from its use of data on other cultures to formulate theories concerning human nature and to investigate the array of human possibilities that are coalesced in different cultural traditions. For example, many textbooks and supplementary readings in American cultural anthropology make the point that we can better understand ourselves by understanding others, or that we must understand the human other in order to understand the totality of human experience. The American anthropologist John Rowe (1965) correctly suggests that modern anthropology is rooted in the Western Renaissance because it was during this period that Western scholars began to contrast their existing culture with extinct cultures of the past, i.e., historical, pagan others, as well as with existing other cultures.

The thesis of this book is that a naturalistic perspective by itself (i.e., to locate humans as part of nature and to have a non-theological discourse on humankind), although necessary, is not sufficient to distinguish the anthropological worldview. Anthropology's uniqueness stems from the use of the human other. Certain cultural structures of meaning in the West validate the use of the human other as a source of knowledge for defining the nature of humankind, culture and society.

I suggest that the cultural structures of meaning which validate the use of the human other derive from the Judeo-Christian orientation of the West. The following paragraphs explore this idea. It should be emphasized that the discussion of the Judeo-Christian orientation in this book attempts to identify some of the *basic cultural structures of meaning*. Particular believers will have personal interpretations that may not be congruent with the cultural patterns that I have identified.

I must also emphasize the fact that I have, for the purpose of this book, selected a particular theme of the Judeo-Christian orientation, namely, that of the Christian conception of the self as it is discussed by scholars such as Hayden White (1972). I am aware of the fact that there are several interpretations of the relationship between humans and the divine in this orientation and that some of the most brilliant minds have dealt with the problem of the Christian self in different ways. My concern is not with the theological controversies but with how the Christian symbol of divinity serves as a vehicle to conceptualize the human self, and the implications of such a conceptualization for the emergence and maintenance of anthropology as a culturally accepted phenomenon.

The Judeo-Christian orientation emphasizes that the true nature of the self should be understood in terms of the true nature of the divine being (see Chapter Four for a discussion of the concept of the self). The self-identify of the Christian is legitimized and made meaningful with reference to the identity of the divine being; the untrue self is composed of attributes that could not be identified as the attributes of the divine being. This contrast in identity formulation is crucial in making the distinction between good and evil, sin and grace, normal and abnormal, order and disorder, etc.

To elucidate the significance of the representation of the divine in a particular manner in the Judeo-Christian orientation, it is useful to compare and contrast this orientation with other orientations. When people have divinities that represent the characteristics and the aspirations of the group, the divinities function as symbols of group identity. The self and group identity are related to and conceptualized with reference to those symbols. All human beings need metaphors of the self for comprehending what the self is. Divinities are often representations of the values considered to be sacred by the group in the Durkheimian sense. These divinities represent the human self as defined by the group, and individuals use them as vehicles to conceptualize their self identity.

The divine beings in the Greek tradition, for example, served as a mirror of human life, and as systems of personal and group integration, and the Greeks used their divinities quite differently from the participants in the Judeo-Christian orientation. Greek divine beings expressed the coexistence of diverse, contradictory elements in human life; they explored the nature of good and evil, virtue and debasement, maleness and femaleness, often depicting the coexistence of opposites in the same divine figure. These divinities were symbols of human experience, and they brought within the Greek conception of the self the great diversity of human possibility; they represented and legitimized the complexity of the human condition. Gorgons, one-eyed witches, giants, heroes who were sometimes cowardly, bad kings who were also good, false wives who were sometimes true— the strange, the abnormal, the bad as well as the good, were all incorporated in a representation of the self.

The Christian orientation, on the other hand, presents an absolutist, restricted representation of divinity as the embodiment of perfection, and hence, in terms of the mirror function of such representations, does not serve as a vehicle to conceptualize the total self in relation to the complexities of human experience. It provides moral prescriptions of goodness and virtue. Excluded from the conception of the true self are all the negative, dark sides of human possibility. The Christian orientation, in other words, rejects the enactment of the complexity of the human condition in the representation of divinity and offers a restricted image of the human self. The vices and the weaknesses are excluded from the conception of the self, and such an exclusion introduces a dichotomy and contrast between the true self and the untrue self.

The Greeks did not claim a universal religion; theirs was a Greek religion, different from the religions of non-Greeks. But within their own group-specific religion they embraced in divine representation the full, contradictory, paradoxical range of human possibility. For the Greeks, the self was full of acceptable contrasts (as represented by their divinities); the self was not dichotomized into a divinely sanctioned true self and a divinely rejected untrue self.

The Judeo-Christian orientation introduced a different structure of meaning into the Western tradition. Christianity claimed to be a universal religion of humankind, embracing all peoples. But within this pan-human scheme, a contrast was made between people who were saved, those with grace, who had a special relationship with God and who participated in the truth, as opposed to those who were out of grace, who were not saved, and who did not participate in the truth. Thus a dichotomy was established between the true self and the untrue self. The true component of the self was that which was linked with the divine being, from whom true knowledge was acquired. This resulted in rejecting or debasing all those human attributes that did not correspond to what was represented as the true nature of the divine being.

Note that the distinction being made here is not the us/other dichotomy of ethnicity but the true-self/untrue-self dichotomy of the Judeo-Christian orientation. All human groups consider themselves special, opposing themselves to other groups. The us/other conception serves as a boundary-maintaining mechanism. In many languages, the word used to identify "us" is "people," thus making a contrast between people and non-people. The Greeks called non-Greeks barbarians because the non-Greeks did not speak Greek.

My thesis identifies a feature of the Western tradition which is different from patterns of boundary-maintenance in all human societies (including the West). In the Judeo-Christian orientation, the representation of divinity embraced all peoples, but created a distinction in the conception of the true self and the untrue self. Anthropology, in continuing this structural principle, embraced humanity as a whole but made the contrast between the West and the non-West which corresponded to the dichotomy between the true self and the untrue self; the West shared in the attributes of the true self.

The anthropological orientation (of using the human others to discuss the nature of humankind) which arose in the late Renaissance carried forward the Judeo-Christian orientation in a number of different ways. The writings of many anthropologically oriented scholars reflected the writings of the Church fathers in conceptualizing the universal history of humankind. In writing the natural history of humankind, Western scholars used the examples of existing non-Western cultures to reconstruct the past. Just as in the Judeo-Christian orientation God was conceptualized as revealing his will in human history through Christians, anthropologically oriented scholars conceptualized the human mind as unfolding itself in greater and greater awareness or perfection through the West. This kind of natural history found its full expression in the writings of the German philosopher Hegel, who was himself a theologian.

The late Renaissance was a period of great religious and social turmoil. It was during this period that the Protestant Reformation occurred, the discovery of the New World began to loom large in the consciousness of the Europeans, justification for the use of African slaves on the basis of physical differences was offered, modern capitalism became systematized, fear of witchcraft was widespread, mysticism as well as experimentation were common, and a mechanistic orientation reemerged. Also, descriptions and interpretations of non-Western peoples became a scholarly activity. The anthropological orientation that we associate with the West developed mostly in those countries in northwestern Europe that became "Protestant," or those that had Protestant cultural currents (although it is true that many Jesuit missionaries did describe the customs of non-Western peoples from the 13th century). The anthropological theories which we discuss are primarily those of the British, the Germans and the Americans, with emphasis on the contributions of the French. Seldom do we hear, in the history of anthropology, of the contributions of Spain, Portugal, Italy or Eastern Europe.

The above comment about Protestantism requires clarification. I have suggested in this book that modern anthropology arose during the late Renaissance and that the combination of non-theological discourse on humankind and the conceptual model of the self of the Judeo-Christian orientation provided the epistemological foundation for modern anthropology. Protestant movements were important intellectual currents in the late Renaissance, and it is possible to discern some interconnectedness between Protestantism and modern anthropology, but this does not mean that there was a causal link between the two.

It is legitimate to consider the possibility that Protestantism provided an impetus for the development of anthropological ideas, just as it has been suggested that Protestantism provided an impetus for the development of modern capitalism as well as modern science. However, my concern in this book is not to identify the specific or distinctive Protestant or Roman Catholic theological controversy as it relates (or does not relate) to modern anthropology. The Judeo-Christian themes such as the contrast between the true self and the untrue self, and the writing of universal history with the revelation of truth through the Christians, go back to the writings of Saint Paul as well as those of Saint Augustine and other Church fathers. (See Hayden White's 1972 essay for a discussion of these Judeo-Christian themes.)

As I have pointed out earlier, the objective of my study is not to introduce any particular interpretation of Christian theology but to identify a particular cultural structure of meaning as it derived from the Judeo-Christian orientation and as it related to the conception of the self in the Western tradition, which, in turn, provided the intellectual, epistemological justification for modern anthropology.

There is recognition within the discipline of anthropology today that anthropology needs to be examined in its historical, cultural, social and political context in order to understand the discipline's limitations, scope and potential. In recent times a number of histories of anthropology have been written, focusing on different aspects that contributed to the emergence of the discipline of anthropology. However, there has been no

systematic attempt to examine anthropology in terms of how it was
accepted in the Western tradition. Various historians of anthropology have
alluded to the linkage between anthropology and Christianity. Hodgen
(1964), for example, has documented the use in anthropology of the
Christian taxonomy, the Great Chain of Being; Stocking, Jr. (1968) has
shown that the Christian historical method served as a model for anthropology; and scholars such as Voget (1975), Gruber (1974) and Kennedy
(1974) have also referred to the connections between early anthropology
and Christianity. But implicit in these writings is the assumption that
however much anthropology may be linked in its early years to Christianity,
modern anthropology is not linked to the Judeo-Christian orientation. I
argue that the linkage exists and that anthropology is accepted in the West
as a valid orientation or mode of understanding because of that linkage.

Toward an Authentic Anthropology

The term "authentic anthropology" has been used by scholars such as
Ernest Becker (1971) and Victor Turner (1974) whose views I discuss briefly
in Chapter Twelve. I suggest that anthropology becomes "authentic" when
it becomes aware of its nature, history and function in the Western tradition. This awareness, I suggest, comes from studying how and why anthropological data were used in a certain manner at certain times, how the use
meets the intellectual, emotional, material needs of a generation, and from
examining our motives in using the anthropological data in a certain
manner.
    To become an "authentic" anthropologist, the anthropologist must
study or analyze her/his own cultural structure, or the structures of
meaning that incorporate the human other, in much the same way that a
psychoanalyst undergoes analysis before analyzing others. I suggest that a
student in anthropology should be trained in philosophy, sociology and
history before undertaking fieldwork and comparative research. All people,
including anthropologists, have the tendency to view themselves as having
learned from the mistakes of their ancestors and to assume that somehow
they are much more scientific and objective in their anthropological
statements. The anthropological racism and fabrications of the 19th
century, for example, are today attributed to the peculiar biases of the
period; it is tacitly assumed that today's anthropologists have cast aside
bias. I suggest that in certain matters, particularly those that involve discussion of peoples, every generation makes the same or similar mistakes as
earlier generations. What the present generation regards as anthropologically scientific statements will be discarded as biased and unscientific by
succeeding generations.
    Rodney Needham once remarked (1980) that the history of scientific

anthropology is a series of mistakes. I suggest that by studying the reasons why and how anthropological data are used to meet the intellectual, material and emotional needs of a generation, anthropologists can reduce the number of mistakes, mistakes that in many instances have had grave consequences for human others.

How does contemporary anthropology function in the Western tradition? Wagner (1975:vii) states:

> Like many other aspects of modern American interpretive culture, anthropology has developed the habit of preempting the means and idioms through which protest and contradiction are expressed and making them a part of its synthetic and culturally supportive message. Exoticism and cultural relativity are the bait, and the assumptions and ideologies of a culture of collective enterprise are the hook that is swallowed with the bait. Anthropology is theorized and taught as an effort to *rationalize* contradiction, paradox, and dialectic, rather than to trace out and realize their implications; students and professionals alike learn to repress and ignore these implications, to "not see" them, and to imagine the most dire consequences as a putative result of not doing so. They repress the dialectic so that they may *be* it.

The establishment of an authentic anthropology could greatly improve anthropology's understanding of its true nature, and the West's understanding of its own cultural orientations which are linked with the discipline of anthropology. I believe that an introductory course in the anthropological academic curriculum titled *Anthropology and the Western Tradition* would be a meaningful entry into the discipline of anthropology. Such a course would involve the examination, interpretation and evaluation of how and why Western scholars have examined, interpreted and evaluated the data on non-Western peoples. It would also sensitize the student to the philosophical, historical and sociological issues related to the development of anthropology as a discipline as well as promote anthropology as a part of humanistic scholarship. I discuss the above views further in the concluding chapter.

Part I
Inventing Human Nature

Human beings generally adopt and enact what is traditionally accepted as natural or appropriate behavior. Only when people engage in self-conscious attempts to understand the determinants of human behavior, or when they cannot accept the definitions of appropriate behavior and try to create alternatives, do they reflect on whether such behavior is natural.

The idea of "human nature" is implicit in discourse on what is considered, or not considered, valid behavior. Social interaction among those who share a common conception of appropriate behavior reinforces the idea that such behavior is somehow "natural," a product of "human nature." The idea of the naturalness of certain behavior is usually linked conceptually with the idea of divinely ordained behavior, which spawns debates on the relationship between divine law, natural law and human law, and the discrepancies between and among them.

The on-going process by which people adopt and enact appropriate behavior (which they implicitly assume to be "natural") may be identified as the internalization and externalization of cultural naturalness, or as *the cultural invention of human nature.* A significant aspect of contemporary anthropology is the study of this process.

Humans approximate their universe with cultural categories and then use them without an awareness that the categories are acquired. To most human beings, proof is demonstrated by the development of their children as they learn to speak a particular language, eat a particular type of food, and acquire selfhood approximating the expected stages of development — in other words, as they develop in a culturally appropriate, particular manner. For those who have shared in this process, such acquisition of behavior is proof that their behavior is natural and that they have a true understanding of human nature.

Anthropology is an attempt to invent human nature through the study of the cultural inventions of human nature. Contemporary anthropology of

15

the past three decades or so, more than in earlier decades, has focused on the study of the non-rational foundations of the cultural inventions of human nature. Such a study involves the examination and analysis of symbol and myth, of meaning and the non-rational in human communication, and their implications for selfhood and social action. This development in anthropology is a reflection of the intellectual developments of the 20th century in the Western tradition: the study of meaning has become a preoccupation not only in the humanities but in the social sciences. Thus, the present orientation in anthropology must be seen as part of the cultural invention of human nature in contemporary Western tradition.

Until about a century ago, anthropologists invented human nature based on assumptions about the progressive use as well as development of rationality in human action. The social institutions of the West were seen as the culmination of the true rational expression of human nature. Contemporary anthropology, to a large extent, eschews these assumptions. Utilitarian, practical concerns are still considered important in causal explanations of cultural change, cultural evolution and the functional interrelatedness of technological, economic, political and religious systems; but there is recognition in contemporary anthropology that human nature must be inferred also from non-rational and symbolic factors that provide coherence and meaning that are crucial for human action in every society.

The linkage of the utilitarian and the symbolic, and the motivating function of the symbolic in human action can be seen in most of the domains of human social action. A few examples should illustrate this fact. The Shakespearean aphorism, "Love reasons without reason," expresses this linkage in the domain of love and marriage. People get married for a variety of reasons, some utilitarian, some for reasons "beyond the range of reason." They may or may not be willing to die for each other, depending on how the relationship symbolizes or represents the self-identity of the participants. In the religious domain, fanatics may die and kill for religious myths and symbols. There may be economic and political reasons generating the conflict, but national-political entities often depend on the mobilizing power of myths and symbols which link territorial integrity with personal or self identity (cf. Pandian 1977). A significant aspect of human nature is invented in contemporary anthropology through the study of myth, symbol, selfhood, and the non-rational foundations of cultures (defined as systems of meaning); I discuss in the next three chapters some of the issues involved in such a study.

Chapter Two

The Teaching of Anthropology

The Anthropology Curriculum in American Academia*

The teaching of anthropology is generally organized in the following manner:

Anthropology (The Study of Humankind)

Physical or Biological Anthropology	Archaeological Anthropology	Linguistic Anthropology	Cultural Anthropology
The study of human evolution, human variation, primate anatomy and behavior	The study of extinct cultures, sequences of cultural history, and epochs	The study of the structure of language, the relationship between language and culture, the use of language in social contexts	The study of culture, also called ethnology, which includes psychological anthropology, social anthropology, structural anthropology and ecological anthropology

Anthropology can also be conceptualized as having two main branches, physical anthropology and cultural anthropology; archaeology and linguistics may be subsumed under cultural anthropology. Some textbooks deal with all branches of anthropology; some cover physical anthropology and archaeology in one volume, and cultural anthropology and linguistics in another; and some texts review only one branch of anthropology because many departments offer four separate introductory courses. Archaeology is sometimes linked with physical anthropology in studies that deal with

*See Mandelbaum, Lasker and Albert (eds.), *The Teaching of Anthropology,* 1967, for a discussion of an anthropology curriculum for college students as it was conceptualized by some of the leading anthropologists of the 1960's.

fossils (paleoanthropology) and sometimes with cultural anthropology in studies which interpret the way of life of extinct cultural traditions (ethno-archaeology). Recent theoretical developments in linguistics and cultural anthropology have brought the two sub-disciplines close together. At a certain level of theoretical formulation, anthropologists try to synthesize the knowledge of all the different branches, and use the concept of culture as the unifying principle of anthropological discourse. Culture in general is humankind's primary mode of adaptation; cultures in particular are the cultural traditions or customs of particular groups. I will discuss the concept of culture in Chapter Three.

In addition to the basic introductory courses, specialized fields of inquiry within the different branches of anthropology are taught as an essential part of the anthropology curriculum; and most departments of anthropology offer a variety of courses that have a comparative focus, such as medical anthropology, urban anthropology, economic anthropology, forensic anthropology, anthropology of religion, anthropology of play, anthropology of law, anthropology of art, anthropology of education, anthropology of cultural change, and anthropology of peasants. Also, depending on the expertise of the departmental faculty, area courses may be offered that deal with peoples of different geographical regions, such as peoples of Africa, peoples of Europe, peoples of Asia, peoples of North America, and peoples of South America. Departments may offer general courses on anthropological theory and method and the history of anthropology, and seminars that deal with specific research topics.

The teaching of anthropology as an undergraduate major is, for the most part, a post-World-War-II phenomenon. Until then, the locus of anthropology was in the museums and the governmental bureaus involved in collecting data about native Americans. Before the war, a few major institutions offered courses in anthropology, and Ph.D.'s were also awarded. Franz Boas, who was a professor of anthropology at Columbia University, began to shape the course of American academic anthropology from the beginning of the 20th century. However, there were not many jobs in academia, and if anthropology courses were offered, they were not necessarily taught by full-time teaching anthropologists because anthropology in most places was affiliated with disciplines such as psychology, sociology, and geography.

Hymes (1969) notes that the post-World-War-II developments in academic anthropology did not necessarily promote the true mission of anthropology. Departments, in their success with high enrollments, job possibilities, and availability of grant money, became baronies or fiefdoms protecting their narrow, parochial, personal interests. On the one hand this led to differentiation and diversity in anthropological approaches, and on the other to vagueness in defining the common objectives and goals of anthropology. Anthropologists engaged in certain types of research because money was available, and pursued personal interests in the name of anthropology. A common professional culture was lost.

Beyond this problem, identified by Hymes, was another problem which many other disciplines besides academic anthropology were also experiencing. As the number of anthropologists increased, communication about ongoing research and contributions became more difficult to achieve. As in other disciplines, specialization occurred; it became uncommon for an anthropologist to be equally knowledgeable in all branches of anthropology. Anthropologists specialized in either the study of culture, human biology, archaeology or language, and communication across the specializations became more difficult because each branch had developed its own jargon and mode of discourse.

A development which began before the war led to the emergence of a distinctive identity of American anthropology, as distinguished from its British, French and German counterparts. The British anthropological tradition of the 20th century broke from the evolutionary anthropology of earlier centuries by making disciplinary distinctions between social anthropology, ethnology and physical anthropology.

The following quote from A.R. Radcliffe-Brown's statement on the nature of social anthropology provides an accurate picture of the conceptual differences between the American and British anthropological traditions:

> A meeting of teachers from Oxford, Cambridge and London was held to discuss the terminology of our subject. We agreed to use "ethnography" as the term for descriptive accounts of non-literate peoples. The hypothetical reconstruction of "history" of such peoples was accepted as the task of ethnology and prehistoric archaeology. The comparative study of the institutions of primitive societies was accepted as the task of social anthropology, and this name was preferred to "sociology."

> Marett proposed that we should make a primary dichotomy between "physical anthropology" and "cultural anthropology" including in the latter ethnology, social anthropology, archaeology and linguistics, and perhaps also folk-lore. One objection to this was that ethnology as the geographical and historical study of peoples and their migrations and interactions, as it was commonly taught, included racial history based on physical anthropology and human paleontology. (Radcliffe-Brown 1952:276)

The French anthropological tradition also made disciplinary distinctions similar to those of the British. Both traditions preferred the use of concepts such as "society," "social structure" and "social institutions," and had a lineal affinity with the writings of the French, Scottish and English social/moral philosophers and institutionalists of the Renaissance and the Enlightenment.

Despite the distinctiveness of social anthropology, it has continued to be an important part of American cultural anthropology; an intense dialogue between the two persists. Robert H. Lowie wrote in 1953 that "Whatever differences may divide cultural from social anthropologists, they are hardly greater than those which divide self-styled cultural anthropologists." British social anthropologists such as A.R. Radcliffe-Brown, E.E. Evans-Pritchard, Raymond Firth, Edmund R. Leach and Rodney Needham, and French social anthropologists such as Marcel Mauss, Claude Levi-Strauss and Louis Dumont, have influenced the theoretical orientation of American cultural anthropology.

The German anthropological tradition also makes a sharp distinction between physical anthropology and ethnology. German ethnologists do not consider valid the American conception of anthropology as a unified field of inquiry in the study of humankind. The German ethnological tradition was shaped by studies in cultural or group psychology, historicism and human geography. German ethnologists in the 20th century sought to identify the origins and diffusion of cultural wholes. Robert Heine-Geldern (1964), in an important article on the history of German ethnology, identified several distinguishing characteristics. Two of his main points are described in the following passage:

1) Ethnology comprises the study of all aspects of human culture, including social organization, economy, law, religion, folklore, mythology, art, music, technology, etc. It comprises also ethno-history....

2) Ethnology is a branch of the humanities (*Geistes-wissenschaften*). It is true that Frobenius, at least during one period of his life, thought that cultures, since he considered them as "living being," should be studied by the methods of the natural sciences. This was, of course, no more than a curious aberration. It is certainly not borne out by his own work. In recent times, only Muhlmann (1938: 91 ss.) thinks that ethnology has a double aspect and belongs to both the humanities and the natural sciences. (Heine-Geldern 1964:416)

German ethnology influenced American cultural anthropology through Franz Boas and others interested in cultural psychology and cultural history. The German tradition emphasized the importance of the concept of culture as does the American tradition. I discuss this point in Chapter Three in greater detail.

American anthropology has retained the unified and holistic scope of anthropology as it was originally conceived, although a few departments have, in recent times, established separate departments of biological anthropology and archaeological anthropology, and have combined cultural anthropology in programs such as "human relations" or "social relations." The integrative nature of anthropology is largely sustained by promoting culture as the central, unifying concept of the discipline of anthropology. The distinctiveness of the human species is in its creating and using culture.

Anthropology as a Holistic Study of Humankind

The Random House Dictionary defines holism as "the theory that whole entities, as fundamental components of reality, have an existence other than as the mere sum of their parts." Anthropological holism refers to the idea that 1) explanations of humankind must take into account biological, mental, social and cultural dimensions and that 2) in the study of human phenomena it is necessary to understand the interconnectedness or functional relations of the components that constitute whole systems. Thus, in discussing any particular dimension of humankind—biological, mental, social or cultural—the anthropologist must look for its relationship with other dimensions.

The holistic approach is anti-reductionist; ideally the anthropologist should reject the explanation of human behavior in terms of simple, isolated elements of biology, mind, social relationships or culture. In actual practice, however, the holistic approach involves complex, cumbersome intellectual effort. Science is an analytic, inductive-deductive process which involves the formulation of theories or generalizations that predict regularities and recurrences of phenomena and identifies empirically verifiable relationships or hypotheses that support or reject such formulations. The relationships among biological, mental, social and cultural variables are, more often than not, understood intuitively to be valid rather than proven scientifically to be true. The holistic approach tends to be used in a negative way: to argue against reductionist theories rather than to provide scientifically valid holistic theories.

Some attempts at formulating holistic theories have been made, however. Psychological and structural anthropologists have related mental and cultural aspects, social anthropologists social and cultural aspects, biological anthropologists biological and cultural aspects, and ecological and medical anthropologists have related biological and environmental factors.

The controversies which surround postulations about human nature and culture may be examined to shed light on the significance of anthropological holism. As stated in the introduction to Part I, most people talk about human behavior in terms of human nature. Behaviors which are disliked or unfamiliar are often considered deviations from human nature. The examination of what is "natural" or "true" in human behavior has a long intellectual tradition of moral, social and natural philosophy in the West, going back to at least the early Greeks. Does human behavior correspond to natural law? Are certain types of human behavior more natural than others? The West has a long tradition of issuing such statements as "man is a social animal," "man is a political animal," "man is innately aggressive," "man is innately spiritual," and so on.

From an anthropological perspective, none of the above statements are, by themselves, valid formulations of human nature. What we regard as natural in human behavior is, according to the anthropologist, a product of our acquiring a symbolic universe, the socially transmitted cultural tradition of a human group. In Chapter Three I will discuss in detail what is meant by symbolic universe, cultural tradition and human group. The main point to be made here is that pronouncements concerning human nature are misleading and can be totally erroneous unless we take into account the reality of culture which is not genetically transmitted. About the only statement we can make about human nature is that it is human nature to acquire culture.

Adequate models do not yet exist that enable us to understand fully the transformation, linkages and correspondences of the elements that derive from or are products of the different dimensions of being human. Into the vacuum of our ignorance about the specifics of these relationships have flowed confusing, often preposterous statements about human nature, many of them issued in the name of science, and many by anthropologists linking language, culture and "race" in explaining human behavior.

Theorists of human nature, particularly those influenced by human sociobiology or the study of the genetic-biological basis of human behavior, have suggested that a variety of behaviors and relationships such as aggression, altruism, polygyny and male bonding are rooted in genes, but so far no one has been able to establish a correspondence. Most anthropologists reject sociobiological theories, pointing out that human behavior is highly variable and flexible, shaped by the historically evolved, distinctive cultural patterns of the society in which a child is enculturated or socialized. Extensive brain development occurs after birth, lengthening the period of human maturation in comparison to that of other mammals, during which time a child is transformed from a non-speaking, non-symbol-bearing organism without rules of human behavior to a human being who can use fluently the symbols of meaning within his society. A child is not born with a particular language, a particular symbol-system, or a set of rules of human behavior. The child is not genetically programmed for any particular cultural form, but is genetically endowed to acquire the forms appropriate to the social context in which he was born. A child born in Asia but raised in Europe will be European in language, belief, values and standards of behavior.

Particular languages, beliefs, values and standards of behavior are external to the human organism, and must be acquired for a human organism to become a human being.

Beyond this universal feature of the human acquisition of culture, there are other cultural universals which anthropologists study in human communities. In the realms of marriage and family, education and recreation, religious belief, and economic and political transactions, anthropologists investigate the shared cultural realities that are transmitted from one generation to another. The content of each of these group activities varies; there are different types of family and kinship systems, different types of politics, economics and religion. Contemporary anthropologists have identified the *recurrence* of certain types and have suggested that we can explain the reasons for such recurrence without invoking the notion of human nature.

Anthropology attempts to explain why there are similarities and differences in the various cultural traditions. Until the beginning of 20th-century anthropology, most anthropologists perceived social institutions as developing because of the principle of progress, which was considered a law of human nature, a biological and/or mental fact. Thus some beliefs and institutions were thought to be more evolved or progressed, and certain "races" were identified as having produced higher or lower forms of beliefs and institutions. Particular institutional orientations such as monogamy and monotheism were considered to be the highest forms of progress and were thought to belong only to the most advanced races. The 20th century dawned with the realization that cultural variation did not correspond with racial variation and that assumptions about progress were fallacious. Contemporary anthropologists consider it spurious to distinguish human groups on a scale of mental and cultural advancement. There is no universally valid yardstick to measure or declare the superiority or inferiority of particular group beliefs or social institutions, no absolute standards for ranking beliefs or institutions as good or bad. The ingredients of culture must be understood in relation to the cultural tradition in which they are accepted as real.

Such conceptions, known as cultural relativism, suggest that the validity of knowledge and morals is relative to the tradition in which they exist. Although relativism of knowledge and morals has been an important concern of many philosophers from ancient times and of the sociologists of knowledge and historicists of recent times, anthropology, by insisting on the viability of different beliefs and institutions for different human groups, became the chief instrument in the Western tradition for promoting understanding of beliefs and institutions of other peoples without imposing value judgments.

Cultural relativism does not undermine our own beliefs and institutions. We hold them to be true and valid because we use them to define our humanity, to behave as humans in the context of our own tradition. Cultural relativism recognizes that other people hold their beliefs and institutions to be true and valid and suggest that we should not undermine them for the sole reason that they are not the ones we use. Cultural relativism helps us to be less ethnocentric, i.e., not to define the total human universe from the perspective of our particular cultural tradition.

Because most contemporary anthropologists hold that the biopsychological make-up of all human groups is essentially similar, biological or psychological factors are not considered the determinants of cultural and social differences. The human organism and the human mind are constants.

Beliefs and institutions must be created by humans, but once created they become external cultural realities. The creation of cultural reality is an on-going process. I discuss this point further in Chapter Three.

The Empirical Study of Cultural and Human Variation

In this section I will comment briefly on the empirical study of cultural and human variation.

Anthropology's distinctiveness in the 20th century is often discussed in terms of the methodology of fieldwork or long-term participant observation of an alien group. Anthropological fieldwork is of recent origin, a 20th-century appendage to the anthropology which developed since the Renaissance. Before the 20th century, anthropologists relied on field notes, reports and travelogues of adventurers, explorers, missionaries and civil servants of colonial governments. Today participant observation is not unique to anthropology. Participant observation is sustained by phenomenological method and the psychology of empathy, although anthropologists committed to positivism often will identify observable behavioral traits as the units of analysis. (See Pandian 1974, 1975a, 1975b).

In recent times anthropologists have occasionally studied their own culture, usually because they were denied access to many non-Western countries. Such studies, however, have provoked extensive debates concerning the merits or difficulties in conducting anthropological fieldwork in one's own society, and are considered not quite as legitimate as the study of a culture which is very different from one's own. It is often pointed out that the anthropologist can be more "objective," or less emotionally involved in the study of an alien culture; and that the experience of being in a different symbolic reality (in which he learns the new cultural and linguistic categories just as a child would learn them) would sensitize the anthropologist to linguistic and cultural relativism. This is seen as a necessary requirement for initiation into the ranks of professional anthropology and professional identity as an anthropologist.

A contrast is often made between the "emic" and "etic" approaches. In the former approach, "native" categories of thought are elicited to identify the logic of symbolic classifications, the principles of organization, etc. A number of recent theoretical trends in anthropology such as ethnoscience or ethnosemantics, symbolic anthropology and semiotic anthropology incorporate the emic methodology.

The etic approach emphasizes the observation of certain types of behavior for the maintenance of social cohesion, a viable relationship with the environment, etc. Ecological and social anthropologists have traditionally been associated with this approach, as have anthropologists who formulate adaptation models of cultural change.

The following quote from Pelto and Pelto (1978:62) illustrates the differences between the two approaches:

Emic	Etic
1. Primary method is interviewing, in depth, in the native language.	Primary method is observation of behavior.
2. Intent is to seek the categories of *meanings,* as nearly as possible in the ways "the natives define things."	Intent is to seek patterns of behavior, as defined by the observer.
3. The people's definitions of meaning, their idea systems, are seen as the most important "causes" or explanations of behavior.	Impersonal, nonideational factors, especially material conditions, are seen as significant movers of human action.
4. Systems and patterns are identified through logical analysis, especially by a quasi-linguistic analysis of contrast sets.	Systems and patterns are identified through quantitative analysis of events and actions.
5. Cross-cultural generalizations must wait for the *conversion* of culturally specific patterns and meanings into more abstracted, intercultural categories.	Cross-cultural generalizations *can* be made directly, by applying the same methods of observation, with the same outside-derived concepts, to two or more different cultures.
6. The methodological strategy is fundamentally inductive, for research cannot proceed until the "'natives' categories of meaning" have been *discovered.*	The methodological strategy can range from "pure induction" to various mixtures of inductive and deductive re-*search.*

The developments in physical anthropology, particularly the recent discoveries of the fossils of the early hominid *Australopithecus afarensis,* dated at over 3 million years old, have raised many questions about the beginning of bipedalism, tool use, language, culture and increased brain size, and the advancements in human populational and molecular genetics have made many physical anthropologists discard the typological classifications and anthropometric measurements once used to discuss human variation.

The mechanism of human variation, that is, the process by which variation originates and is maintained, has been extensively investigated by human geneticists and physical anthropologists. The accumulating corpus of research has prompted many biologists and anthropologists to suggest that the concept of race and racial categories are fallacious and misleading. The concept of race, in the sense of a distinctive, fixed population, the individual members of which all share a particular package of traits, imposes on the flow of genetic events a boundary, uniformity and continuity which does not actually exist. A closer approximation of the facts of human variation is achieved through clinal analysis, by charting the frequency of isolated biological traits and developing causal hypotheses which relate the occurrence of particular traits to nutritional, climatic and other variables (cf. Chapter Eight).

The development of the use of the concept of race in anthropology is in many ways similar to the development of Ptolemaic astronomy. Ptolemaic astronomy was based on the assumption that heavenly bodies moved around the earth on crystalline spheres. The number of spheres required to explain the erratic movements of the planets became so numerous that as an explanatory device the sphere became absurd. In like manner, the theory of race is predicated on the assumption that there are pure races. Most biological anthropologists begin with three or four racial categories but are then forced to develop numerous subcategories to explain erratic populations which do not fit these main categories. It is conceivable that some enthusiastic classifier, wallowing in the data of human diversity, might ultimately propose a million or more racial categories; but his efforts would be as absurd as the Ptolemaic astronomer who, in his careful perusal of the heavens, spots yet another gyration in the heavenly bodies which requires yet another handful of crystalline spheres to "explain" it.

Continuity and Change

There is a two-fold continuity in the history of anthropology. (1) Anthropologists have always used the philosophical, sociological, psychological, biological and linguistic assumptions and theories that developed within the Western tradition. The historian Margaret Hodgen (1964) in her review of anthropological ideas concluded that 19th-century anthropology was "old wine in a new bottle," or little more than a reformulation of Greek, Christian and Renaissance views. The anthropologist Francis L.K. Hsu (1973) lamented that there was "prejudice" in the 20th-century formulations of anthropological theory in the sense that Western anthropologists failed to consider non-Western theoretical formulations of humankind and culture. These continuities exist because anthropology is rooted in the Western cultural structures of meaning, and anthropological discourse would not make sense without reference to the prevailing philosophical, sociological, biological, and linguistic paradigms of the Western tradition.

(2) Since the time of the late Renaissance when modern anthropology developed, anthropologists have continued to use the human other to theorize about human unity and differentness. Anthropology has served the function of mediating between us and the other, resolving the contradiction(s) between the true self and the untrue self through anthropological models of human integration.

Recent concerns about promoting "world anthropology" through journals such as *Current Anthropology* and the emergence of "native" anthropologists who might wish to non-Westernize anthropology may remove anthropology from its roots, i.e., the Western epistemological context. To do so would probably obliterate the difference between anthropology and other disciplinary orientations such as sociology and political science which are also at certain levels comparative and holistic. Furthermore, if we move what we call anthropology from its epistemological context, something analogous to anthropology would be reborn (as Claude Levi-Strauss noted) because anthropology (or whatever else it may be called in the future) has a specific function in the Western tradition, a function rooted in the Judeo-Christian orientation.

It may be pointed out, as Dell Hymes (1969) has done, that there is little uniformity in the manner in which the advanced curriculum in anthropology is organized in the various departments of academic anthropology. Depending on the personal research interests of particular anthropologists and the availability of research funds to meet specific social needs, the theoretical foci and courses taught vary from department to department. Also, there has been a proliferation of sub-sub-specializations that has often made it difficult to carry on a common anthropological dialogue among colleagues and students in the same department. The subject of culture has, however, continued to be a major area of theoretical debate. I discuss some of these debates in the next chapter.

Chapter Three

Culture, Symbol and Myth

The Development of Theoretical Formulations
About Culture in the Western Tradition

The theoretical formulation and refinement of the concept of culture are, to a large extent, related to the development of anthropology, although, as I will point out later, the study of culture is neither confined to the discipline of anthropology nor to the Western tradition.

Kroeber and Kluckhohn (1952:3) note that "...few intellectuals will challenge the statement that the idea of culture, in the technical anthropological sense, is one of the key notions of contemporary American thought." The British anthropologist Edward Tylor who, in 1871, formulated one of the most widely quoted definitions of culture, and American anthropologists such as Franz Boas, Alfred Kroeber, Robert Lowie, Clyde Kluckhohn, Ruth Benedict, Leslie White, Margaret Mead, Clifford Geertz and many other anthropologists of this century, have contributed substantially to the study of culture and to the theoretical refinement of the concept of culture, and these contributions have been widely used in other disciplines such as sociology and history.

In discussing the history of the concept of culture in the Western tradition, it is necessary to distinguish seven different historical linkages: (1) the Latin denotation of *cultus* or cultivation and the connotation of refinement in general; (2) the notion of custom or habit from Middle English *custome,* which derives from Old French *costume* and ultimately from Latin *consuetedo*; (3) the 18th-century empiricist theory of knowledge; (4) the 18th-century German theory of *kultur*; (5) the 18th-century French theory of civilization; (6) the 18th- and 19th- century theories of the evolution of social institutions; and (7) the 20th-century theory of particular cultural traditions.

(1) The use of the word culture, Kroeber and Kuckhohn (1952:283) point out, "...goes back to classical or perhaps pre-classical Latin with the meaning of cultivation or nurture, as it still persists in terms like agriculture,

horticulture, cult, cultus..." Also, it was used to connote refinement through education, as in suggesting that "a person is cultured."

(2) The Greco-Roman tradition of describing other peoples for amusement and administration recognized the diversity of customs. For example, Herodotus' (484-425) *Histories* and Cornelius Tacitus' (55-117) *Germania* describe the diversity of customs. The Roman philosopher and statesman *Boethius* (475-525) in his *Consolation of Philosophy* (tr. 1943) noted that "The customs and laws of diverse nations do so much differ that the same thing which some commend as laudable, others condemn as deserving punishment." The diversity of customs was noted during the Middle Ages: there were descriptions of Muslim (Arab, Mongol and Turk) customs, and travellers such as Marco Polo (1254-1324) also dealt with the customs of other peoples. Sebastian Muenster's (1489-1552) *Cosmographia* (1544) and many other such books described alien customs, focusing upon the abnormal and unusual. The description and discussion of Native American customs became an important aspect of the intellectual tradition of the late Renaissance. For example, Michel de Montaigne (1533-1592) in his *Essays* (1588) compared and contrasted the customs of different peoples.

(3) The philosophy of empiricism, particularly that of John Locke (1632-1704) and his dictum, *tabula rasa,* that the mind was born as an empty slate on which the world as experienced by the five senses was inscribed and processed by reflective thinking, provided a powerful foundation for theorizing about the role of socialization, and in turn for understanding customs as realities that were not genetically transmitted (cf. Harris 1968).

(4) The 18th-century German intellectual movement promoted the notion of *kultur* as a spiritual, intellectual genius of a people. As Elias (1978:4-5) notes:

> The word through which Germans interpret themselves, which more than any other expresses their pride in their own achievement and their own being, is *kultur.*

> The specifically German sense of the concept of *kultur* finds its clearest expression in its derivative, the adjective *kulturell,* which describes the value and character of particular human products rather than the intrinsic value of a person.

The concept of *kultur* is an idealization and glorification of the mind, spirit or soul of a people: "...the German concept of *kultur* places special stress on national differences and the particular identity of groups; primarily by virtue of this, it has acquired in such fields as ethnological and anthropological research a significance far beyond the German linguistic area and the situation in which it originated." (Elias 1978:5)

Why did the concept of *kultur* gain such significance? Elias suggests that it was promoted by the German intelligentsia, who were reacting against the German upper class. The German upper class had adopted the French customs which dominated the style of life of the nobility of Europe and had transcended German nationalism. The intellectuals proceeded to conceptualize and generate a consciousness of what they believed to be the true German character, uniting all German-speaking people into a single national entity. Philosophers, theologians, poets, anthropologists and all men of letters in one way or another contributed to the forging of the idealization and glorification of what was believed to be the German psyche. Elias (1978: 27) observes:

> The peculiar fate of the German bourgeoisie, its political impotence, and the late unification of the nation acted continuously in one direction, reinforcing concepts and ideals [such as *kultur*]...Thus the development of the concept of *kultur* and the ideals it embodied reflected the German intelligentsia without a significant social hinterland....

(5) In his historical survey of the use of the concept of civilization, Elias (1978:30) points out that by the 18th century, the concept was "unequivocally linked with the image of the Frenchman." Furthermore, the concept connoted class differences, contrasting the upper class from the other classes, with French customs constituting the upperclass way of life. The word civilization is derived from the Latin *civis, civilitas*. To the German intellectuals, civilization (*Zivilisation*) meant formalism and practically useful technological knowledge, but it lacked existential authenticity. To quote Elias (1978:43):

> [The] whole survey shows very clearly one thing which is important in this context: whereas the middle classes already played a political role in France at this time [the 18th century], in Germany they did not. In Germany the intellectual status is confined to the sphere of mind and ideas; in France, along with all the other human questions, social, economic, administrative, and political issues come within the range of interests of the courtly/middle-class intelligentsia.

The important difference between the German concept of *kultur* and the French concept of *civilization* was that whereas the former was the expression of the inner essence of a people or nation, the latter was a process in which people participated. To the 18th-century French and to some extent to the 18th-century English, civilization connoted progress; anyone could participate in civilization through cultivation of the faculty of reason and through emulation, training and education. Thus, civilization was not a specific, national attribute; the upper class was the model of aspiration toward progress. At the same time, the concept also denoted stages of human progress, with the category of civilization identified as the highest form and as having superior social institutions. In the 19th century, the concept identified civilization as the product of innately superior people.

Contemporary scholars use the terms culture and civilization interchangeably, but use the latter term more often to identify "complex" societies with urban centers and literary traditions. In general, contemporary French and British scholars prefer the use of concepts such as society and civilization, whereas German and American scholars more frequently use the terms culture and cultural tradition.

(6) The 18th- and 19th-century theories of the evolution of social institutions differed in one respect. The 18th-century scholars, in attempting to answer why a similar mental structure (the human mind) produced diversity in social institutions, concluded that all humans had the capacity to participate in the institutions of civilization but that many had not attained civilized institutions by themselves because they lacked experience and had not applied reason properly. Civilized institutions were expressions of cultivated rationality. Nineteenth-century scholars theorized that the human mind at different stages of development produced different customs or social institutions, and that civilization was the expression of the most highly developed mind. The mind of those who produced civilized institutions was innately more rational.

(7) The 20th-century theory of cultural tradition is an extension of the German idea of *kultur* as it was developed in the United States by Franz Boas and his students. As opposed to the evolutionary scholars of the previous two centuries who spoke of the universal evolutionary stages of human institutions, Boas sought to describe how particular human groups acquired and used their beliefs, values, institutions, technology, etc. These latter were identified as "culture traits"; and the study of their temporal and spatial distributions, their unity as a cultural whole, and their transmission from one generation to another became the major concern of American cultural anthropology. The emic approach, discussed in Chapter Two, became a major mode of cultural analysis in American cultural anthropology.

To Franz Boas and his students, differences among groups in terms of their cultural traits did not imply differences in innate superiority or inferiority of their respective minds. The differences were historically shaped by the opportunities which different groups had in developing and borrowing traits. Once the traits became established, however, they became for the groups the accepted, "true" way of life. Elvin Hatch (1973), in his book *Theories of Man and Culture,* correctly points out that Franz Boas and his students differed significantly from the 19th-century anthropologists such as Edward Tylor:

> Boas' rejection of the European standard of rationality in anthropological analysis was accompanied by an innovation that was a central element in the turn-of-the-century revolution in social thought. In the place of reason as the basis of human institutions, Boas substituted emotion. (Hatch 1973:53)

This view of behavior entails a dramatic shift in the interpretation of the meaning of Western European social institutions, such as Western standards of morality, democracy, and the like. To Tylor and the other evolutionists, these institutions were historical summits, the highest expression so far of the application of reason to social affairs. To Boas, they were simply habitual patterns which Western peoples had grown accustomed to, and the arguments of churchmen and others about their objective reasonableness were illusory. (Hatch 1973: 55)

The Debates and Controversies Concerning the Conceptualization of Culture

As noted earlier, Edward Tylor in 1871 formulated a standard definition of culture. He used the terms culture and civilization synonymously, and he had a universalistic assumption about culture and cultural evolution. In other words, he, like others of the 19th century, theorized about the culture of humankind—how it came into being and how it developed. His definition was as follows (Tylor 1871):

> Culture, or civilization, taken in its wide ethnographic sense, is that complex whole which includes knowledge, belief, art, morals, law, custom, and any other capabilities and habits acquired by man as a member of society.

Contemporary anthropologists agree that two levels of discourse exist in the study of culture. At one level, we examine the cultural tradition, the unique patterns: the organizing principles, the symbols, myths, institutions, technology, etc. which an individual acquires or learns as a member of that tradition. At another level we try to understand the nature of culture in general.

Debates and controversies surround the definition and theoretical formulations of culture because anthropologists in general are divided into those who view culture as an independent reality with its own distinguishable structures and those who view culture as an aspect of the mental structures that produce it. Also, anthropologists are divided into those who focus on the utilitarian and rational foundations of culture, and those who focus on the non-rational, symbolic systems of meaning.

In order to illustrate the above statement, I will discuss the views of the American anthropologist Leslie White who, for more than three decades, engaged in a dialogue with his colleagues on the question of the nature of culture. Alfred Kroeber, in an early paper entitled "The Superorganic" (1917), expressed a view of culture similar to that of Leslie White, and it evoked several critical comments, particularly from Sapir (1917).

Reacting to Kroeber and Kluckhohn's book entitled *Culture: A Critical Review of Concepts and Definitions* (1952) in which the authors stated that

"Culture is an abstract description of trends toward uniformity in the words, acts, and artifacts of human groups," Leslie White (1959:224) had this to say:

> There is...a disturbing lack of agreement as to what they mean by [culture]. To some, culture is learned behavior. To others, it is not behavior at all, but an abstraction from behavior—whatever that is. Stone axes and pottery bowls are culture to some anthropologists, but no material object can be culture to others. Culture exists only in the mind, according to some; it consists of observable things and events in the external world to others. Some anthropologists think of culture as consisting of ideas, but they are divided upon the question of their locus: some say they are in the minds of the peoples studied, others hold that they are in the minds of ethnologists. We go on to "culture is a psychic defense mechanism," "culture is a Rorschach of a society," and so on, to confusion and bewilderment.

White defines culture as "a class of things and events, dependent upon symboling, considered in an extrasomatic context." Symboling is the unique characteristic of *Homo sapiens sapiens,* and the study of the products of symboling in terms of how they determine human behavior is the province of cultural anthropology, or what he calls culturology.

Many anthropologists, while accepting White's thesis that culture is a humanly created reality which is non-genetically transmitted and used as the human mode of adaptation in the physical universe, suggest that the study of culture as a thing by itself with its own laws of existence and evolution is not feasible. For example, Anthony F.C. Wallace (1970:4) states that "It is about as meaningful to claim that 'culture must be explained in terms of culture,' leaving out biological and psychological levels of explanation, as to assert that 'life must be explained in terms of life' without reference to chemistry and physics."

White, however, is talking about culturology as a level of analysis. A biologist can discuss the principles of biological adaptation without discussing the laws of chemistry and physics. In like manner, a culturologist can analyze culture without discussing psychology. Just as organisms could not exist without molecules, culture could not exist without the human mind; but molecules and mind are assumed to be constants, and not the subjects of the biologist's and culturologist's respective modes of inquiry.

The difference between psychological analysis and cultural analysis is in the kinds of questions that are asked. The same phenomenon will yield different answers depending on the questions asked. Emile Durkheim, the French sociologist of the late 19th and early 20th century, made a similar argument in his books about the importance of establishing a level of sociological inquiry independent of psychological and biological inquiry. For example, in talking about suicide, a psychologist would ask why an individual commits suicide. The sociologist, on the other hand, would ask why suicides occur more in one type of society than in another. The sociologist would identify the social factors that contribute to suicide rate, the psychologist the psychological factors which predispose a particular individual to commit suicide.

The anthropologist, in asking why the institutions of couvade or mother-in-law taboo exist, is not concerned, as a culturologist, with whether the husband feels good or bad, or whether the son-in-law feels resentful or anxious, but would try to understand the role which these institutions play in promoting solidarity, and how they functionally fit with other institutions that are meaningful to the participants in that society.

Not all anthropologists accept White's view of culture, nor do they agree that culturological analysis should constitute anthropology.

Psychological anthropologists focus on the relationship between personality and culture, how individuals in the process of socialization begin to organize their experience using cultural categories. Some psychological anthropologists emphasize the uniform personality configuration which results from certain socialization procedures which in turn generates a common cultural configuration—what Wallace (1970) has called an emphasis on "replication of uniformity." Other psychological anthropologists, such as Wallace himself, focus on the "organization of diversity." Wallace (1970) has argued convincingly that cognitive and motivational nonsharing has adaptive significance for any sociocultural system. Complete or total cognitive and motivational sharing is never attained by any sociocultural system. Even the so-called simple, homogeneous cultures are not homogeneous with respect to all their members having a similar or identical mental map. Wallace explains that cognitive uniformity is dysfunctional to sociocultural systems. Knowing fully each other's motivations and cognitions is operationally counterproductive, and if cognitive uniformity is a prerequisite, it would severely handicap a system because the survival of a system would depend on the humanly impossible feat of everyone in the system knowing it in its entirety. Human beings function in a system with what Wallace refers to as "equivalence structure models" that permit them to participate in the system by predicting each other's behavior without having to cognitively or motivationally replicate themselves.

Structural anthropology which is associated with Claude Levi-Strauss's attempts to reveal the logical structure of thought that produces culture. It is assumed that the infrastructures of culture and language are similar at the unconscious level; Levi-Strauss is concerned with identifying the ethnographic transformations of these structures in his efforts to make inferences about the nature of the mind. In recent times, he has suggested that a new orientation like the "science of signs" or "semiology" might emerge to study human communication and information processing. Levi-Strauss is not alone in using the language analogue in the analysis of culture, nor is he alone in promoting various forms of structural and semantic anthropology.

Some scholars, when disagreeing with his methods and his philosophical pronouncements concerning the nature of mind, have focused on the study of "sign-vehicles" and symbolic significations within a methodological framework which is often called semiotics. Umberto Eco (1979:27), for example, "makes semiotics a substitute for cultural anthropology," and Clifford Geertz (1973) identifies his mode of interpretation of cultures as semiotic in orientation.

Although I am in sympathy with this orientation, I also agree with Ioan Lewis (1977:1) when he states:

> In our mass-media obsessed world, it is not surprising that this quasi-linguistic character of symbolism should have received so much attention. Thus following the linguist Saussure's pioneering work, in anthropology, Levi-Strauss's light-footed structuralism and its ponderous American counterpart, *Cognitive Anthropology,* have assumed the burden of decoding the precious messages concealed in arcane symbolism. In the wider world of literature, art and philosophy, fortified by a liberal infusion of phenomenology, the same approach is celebrated in the fashionable craze for Semiotics.

Clifford Geertz and others identified as symbolic anthropologists, although to some extent influenced by structural anthropology, differ from the structural anthropologists in their cultural analysis. According to Geertz, anthropologists should try to understand the meaning of symbols and how people use them in different social contexts. He takes issue with the American structural anthropologists who claim to approximate the cognitive categories and logical classifications of different cultures.

> "A society's culture," to quote Goodenough...in a passage which has become the *locus classicus* of the whole movement, "consists of whatever it is one has to know or believe in order to operate in a manner acceptable to its members." And from this view of what culture is follows a view, equally assured, of what describing it is—the writing out of systematic rules, an ethnographic algorithm, which, if followed, would make it possible so to operate, to pass (physical appearance aside) for a native. In such a way, extreme subjectivism is married to extreme formalism, with the expected result: an explosion of debate as to whether particular analyses (which come in the form of taxonomies, paradigms, tables, trees, and other ingenuities) reflect what the natives "really" think or are merely clever simulations, logically equivalent but substantively different, of what they think. (Geertz 1973:11)

Ongoing throughout American cultural anthropology's history has been a debate about whether the anthropologist should try to elucidate the bio-psychological determinants of culture, or whether he should concentrate on the cultural determinants of human behavior. The latest and most widely publicized round in this debate has been between Margaret Mead (represented posthumously by her writings) and Derek Freeman. Freeman's book,

*Margaret Mead and Samoa: The Making and Unmaking of an Anthro-
pological Myth* (1983), makes two points, one challenging the objectivity of
Mead's ethnographies, and the other attacking the philosophy of cultural
determinism. I discuss the former in Chapter Nine of this book. With
regard to the latter point, Freeman (1983:302) argues that anthropologists
must deal with both biopsychological and cultural foundations of human
behavior:

> ...the doctrine of cultural determinism was formulated in the second
> decade of the twentieth century in deliberate reaction to the equally un-
> scientific doctrine of extreme biological determinism. We may thus
> identify biological determinism as the thesis to which cultural deter-
> minism was the antithesis. The time is now conspicuously due, in both
> anthropology and biology, for a synthesis in which there will be, in the
> study of human behavior, recognition of the radical importance of both
> the genetic and exogenetic and their interaction, both in the past history
> of human species and in our problematic future.

In recent times a broad division has emerged in the theoretical discourse
concerning the nature of culture. Marvin Harris (1968, 1979) has identified
the division as a philosophical disagreement, a divergence in epistemology
that separates anthropologists into two camps, namely, cultural idealism
and cultural materialism. Cultural idealists are those anthropologists who
take into account human intentionality, motivation and meaning, as well as
the cognitive categories. Cultural materialists are those who use the
adaptive model of biology, examine how environmental, technological and
economic factors shape the political and religious ideologies, and are more
concerned with actual behavior and its consequences than with what people
think about their behavior.

Symbol and Myth

In a book entitled *Islam Observed,* Geertz (1968:95) notes:

> There has been, in short, a general shift in modern anthropological dis-
> cussion of culture, and within it of religion as part of culture, a shift
> from a concern with thought as an inner mental state or stream of such
> states to a concern with thought as the utilization by individuals in soci-
> ety of public, historically created vehicles of reasoning, perception, feel-
> ing, and understanding — symbols in the broadest sense of the term.

Webster's New Twentieth Century Dictionary (1979) defines symbol as
follows:

> symbol, n. [Fr. *symbole*; L. *symbolum;* Gr. *symbolon,* a token, pledge,
> sign by which one infers a thing, from *symballein,* to throw together,
> compare; *syn,* together, and *ballein,* to throw.] 1. something that stands

for or represents another thing; especially, an object used to represent something abstract; an emblem; as, the dove is a *symbol* of peace, the cross is the *symbol* of Christianity. 2. a written or printed mark, letter, abbreviation, etc. standing for an object, quality, process, quantity, etc., as in music, mathematics, or chemistry. 3. in psychoanalysis, an act or object representing an unconscious desire that has been repressed. 4. in theology, an abstract or compendium, creed, or a summary of the articles of religion. *Syn.* —type, sign, image, emblem, representation.

The study of symbols involves scholars of many different disciplines with diverse theoretical viewpoints, and has a long history in the Western tradition. The study of symbols and meaning has engaged the attention of contemporary anthropologists, a shift from an earlier emphasis on discovering the laws of culture and analyzing regularities and the recurrence of social phenomena. Raymond Firth (1973), in his book *Symbols: Public and Private,* discusses the history of anthropological interest in the study of symbols and provides a summary of some of the contemporary approaches to the study of symbols in anthropology.

In the following paragraphs I discuss the particular interpretations of the symbol which are used in this book.

People everywhere use representations, or symbols, and connect them to create meaning-systems. These are shared, or public, and are used in everyday intellectual discourse and social interaction as well as in mythological discourse and ritual action. I am concerned with identifying certain symbols, namely, the symbols of human others, and with identifying the structure of meaning, i.e., the cultural structure, that incorporates the human other in the Western tradition. In Chapters Five and Six I discuss in detail the Western cultural structure which incorporates the abnormal other and the fossil other; in Chapters Seven, Eight and Nine I discuss three symbols of the humanities that are used in intellectual discourse and social interaction in the Western tradition.

In any cultural tradition, certain symbols come to acquire greater significance or importance. These symbols serve as major instruments or vehicles for conceptualization and as major affective models that motivate people to act in a certain way; they have greater cognitive and emotive function. From the user's perspective, they have complex, internal associations and at one level become metaphors. These symbols are abstract models which fuse past, present and future: they store meaning as experienced in the past, convey meaning for action, and project images of the future. As Firth (1973:81) states:

> Symbols, as stores of meaning, help to cope with problems of communication over time, aiding recall and obviating to some extent a need for reformulation of ideas. As such they are a cultural asset. Condensation, the encapsulation of many forms, or many meanings, in one sym-

bol by processes of contraction, suppression, transformation, can also
facilitate communication by giving a common reference point for a variety of originally disparate ideas.

The above statements concerning significant symbols can be understood
by reflecting on our personal experiences of communication and social
action, as well as by examining the nature of what we frequently refer to as
"role models."

In the history of a cultural tradition, certain events, objects, or individuals acquire great significance; they are used again and again in discussion and action in a variety of domains. In conceptualizing notions such as
justice, freedom, courage, betrayal, loyalty, superiority, inferiority, success
and failure, and in discussing the meaning of death and related subjects,
certain events, objects and individuals become relevant aids or vehicles. The
events, objects and individuals thus used are inventions or creations in the
sense that various attributes derived from different domains of experience
are associated with them. In one way or another they fuse domains of thinking and action; what is conceptualized becomes applicable in the domain of
action and what is acted out becomes applicable in the domain of thinking.
People become intellectually and emotionally involved with these symbols.

Such symbols have multiple meanings, and people selectively deploy
some or all of their content in different social contexts. The referents of
these symbols can change: in other words, the inventions or creations that
are made in reference to particular events, objects or individuals can be
transferred to other events, objects or individuals. The connotations can
also change. (See Pandian 1981, 1983b.)

The three symbols I discuss in this book, namely, the savage other, the
black other, and the ethnographic other, have, in their specific connotations, different referents in the Western tradition. The symbol of the savage
has a long history; the concrete form of the savage was, at one time, the
primal man, and it changed from the wild man of the forest during medieval
times to the native Americans during colonial times. Cannibalism,
abnormal physical features, insatiable sexuality and other attributes were
associated with the symbol of the savage. The connotations of the savage included the positive noble savage and the negative ignoble savage. As an aid
in conception, the symbol was used to conceive of irrationality, disorder,
chaos, and so on; and as a model for action, the symbol made it legitimate
to take away the land of native Americans. The symbol of the black other is
also ancient, but gradually the sub-Saharan Africans became the primary
referent. The symbol of the black other, as manifested specifically in sub-
Saharan Africans, was used to conceptualize about race or racial inferiority
and superiority, and to justify enslavement. The symbol of the
ethnographic other had different referents and different meanings.

The symbols, with multiple meanings and referents used in different
domains, can be identified readily. They recur in several domains of

thought and action. Scholars have theorized about these symbols in different ways and have labelled them variously as "significant symbols," "core symbols," "master symbols," "key symbols," "central symbols," "dominant symbols," "conceptual-affective models" and so forth.

Sherry Ortner (1973), in her paper "On Key Symbols," distinguishes two types of key symbols, namely, summarizing and elaborating symbols. Summarizing symbols "synthesize or 'collapse' complex experiences and relate the respondent to the grounds of the system as a whole." Elaborate symbols contribute to "the ordering or 'sorting out' of experience."

Ortner identifies two types of elaborate symbols. Some elaborate symbols are for "the ordering of conceptual experience" and some are for "the ordering of action" that "includes key scenarios, or elements of scenarios which are crucial to the means-end relationship postulated in the complete scenario."

Extending her line of thinking, I suggest that certain symbols become metaphors and are by themselves myths. The symbols I discuss in later chapters function as myths.

The word myth is frequently used to mean that a statement is unreal, not factual, just as the word "symbolic" is often used to mean "token action." Neither of these usages is valid. Symbol and myth are valid not because they are factual or non-factual but because they are believed to be true and because they convey a certain kind of meaning necessary to engage in intellectual discourse, social interaction and other action domains.

The word myth is often identified as part of religious systems, but this is misleading because a religious myth can function as a political myth, economic myth, or kinship myth, just as political, economic and kinship myths can function as religious myths. The Aryan myth is a good example to illustrate the nature of myths. It is a religious, political, economic, kinship myth, as well as a "scientific-anthropological" myth. The Aryan myth is a narrative, with a religious and scientific message.

We can define myth as a system of meaning containing information which is empirically both verifiable and non-verifiable. Its validity is in its use to derive meaning. Myths often incorporate verifiable facts, but their efficacy as a meaning-system derives not from their empirical validity but from their use as mediating models of meaning that promote personal and group integration. Myths mediate between different levels of experiential and non-experiential reality, and provide coherent statements on the nature of reality, self, etc. for the believers who accept the statements to be true.

Scholars have often speculated that myth is a product of primitive, irrational, pre-logical mentality. The implication of this speculation is that human progress leads to the progressive elimination of myths, and that scientific understanding will render myths unnecessary. Modernity is opposed to tradition and primitivism, and the modern West is seen as having little use for myths.

The above line of reasoning is fallacious. All human beings, whether they are part of the "modern West" or the "non-modern non-West," use myths, just as all human beings use science. Both mythological and scientific discourse and activity are pan-human universals. Science is analytic, discursive, atomistic and materialistic. Myth is synthetic, presentistic, holistic and idealistic. Whereas science denotes the existence of a reality independent of human consciousness, myth incorporates scientific knowledge and achieves an integration for the individual and group who use it by rendering the information coherent and meaningful for human existence. See Chapter Eleven in which I offer an interpretation of the role of science and the humanities.

Myths have been analyzed as survivals of the irrational, primitive past, as allegories, as social charters, as expressions of unconscious/subconscious wishes, etc. A fruitful line of inquiry was begun by the French structural anthropologist, Claude Levi-Strauss, who suggests that myths are logical mediating models which help people cope with the contradictions and logical inconsistencies that exist in every culture. Myths make tolerable an existence fraught with perplexing dilemmas of love and hate, permanence and change, and so on, by conveying the message that contradictions do not make human life futile. Myths provide the message that the contradictions that are seen in one domain can be compared to contradictions in another domain.

I suggest in this book that different cultural traditions have either restrictive and closed mythic systems, or unrestrictive and open mythic systems. In many traditions, myths deal with the full range of human possibilities. The contradictions experienced by the individual are enacted by mythical characters who fuse the contradictions, and the mythical characters are neither the ideals of perfection nor embodiments of evil: weakness and strength, sexuality and asceticism, love and hatred, are all dramatized in such myths.

I suggest in this book that the Judeo-Christian myths are limited and restrictive in their representation of human possibilities. All that is considered to be bad is left out in the representation of the divine being, and the true self is linked with this perfect being. I suggest that the human other is introduced into the Western tradition as a mythic representation of human possibilities to meet a need which the Judeo-Christian myths do not meet.

I use the term mythology to characterize the emic discourse on myths. Myths could be narratives on the creation of humankind, divine beings, the self, historical claims for land, etc. Mythologies are to some extent exegeses of these narratives and to some extent "rational" explanations of them.

Chapter Four

The Construction of the Self and the
Formulation of Ethnic Identity

To know oneself is to foresee oneself;
to foresee oneself amounts to playing a part.
— Valery

The Mythology of the Self

The self, from the anthropological point of view, is a cultural creation. While philosophers debate the ultimate reality of the self and psychologists discuss the self as mind, ego, or intra-psychic processes, anthropological and sociological approaches are concerned with the symbols, metaphors and models that serve as aids, vehicles or analogues for the conception of the self. A child is not born with a conception of the self, but acquires the public or socially available symbols that refer to or signify similarities and differences among human beings and that connote the significance of human existence. The symbols and concepts provide the foundation for myths about the self, and these myths are often part of religious, political or other aspects of a culture.

Every human society has a tradition of discourse on the subject of the self; such discourse constitutes the mythology of the self. A study of myths about the self, and the mythology of the self, can reveal the world views, values and themes that are part of the cultural tradition to which a person belongs. The conceptions of the self often reflect what is regarded as important in a society because they are derived from, or analogous to, the significant symbols of the culture.

Beginning with the seminal writings of George H. Mead (1934), a large body of knowledge has accumulated concerning the symbolic representation of the "self as object." Sociologists described as "symbolic interactionists" have examined the effects of contexts of social interaction

41

on changes in self image, and on the creation, maintenance and re-creation of the self. It is beyond the scope of this book to discuss these views at length. My concern is to understand a particular type of religious orientation, the Judeo-Christian orientation, which, as I have suggested, creates a dichotomy in the construction of the self.

All religious orientations include myths and mythologies of the self. Because religious orientations explain to the believers truths about human creation, suffering, evil, death, and so on, they play a primary role in the conceptualization of the self in most societies. The self is constantly bombarded by experiences that threaten the integrity of the self. For most people, religious symbols provide the means by which the integrity of the self can be sustained (cf. Geertz 1969).

The religious symbols that aid in the conceptualization of the self vary in terms of how they represent the range of human potentials and possibilities. Some religious symbols are limited, restrictive and closed in the selection of characteristics considered valid or sacred, and other religious symbols function as symbols of experience with which believers can readily identify in relation to their own multifold experiences that include a great range of human potentialities and possibilities. The former symbols lead people to deny or reject some of their own experiences and characteristics, to consider them not a valid part of the self; the latter casts a broader shadow of symbolic validation over the tangled skein of human life. The ·religious symbols of the Judeo-Christian orientation belong to the former category.

The god of Christians is a representation of maleness, perfection, omnipotence, etc. Man is symbolized as created in the image of god. The discrepancy between the perfect god and his imperfect creation is explained in various myths that narrate the fall of man, original sin, salvation, grace, etc. The human experiences and characteristics that cannot be conceptualized with reference to god are identified as evil or abnormal and rejected as aspects of the self not connected with god. Thus a contrast between the true self and the untrue self is made, a contrast which is homologous to the contrast between grace and sin, orthodoxy and heresy, normal and abnormal, goodness and evil, holy and unholy, true knowledge and blasphemy, and so on (cf. White 1972).

From the late Renaissance, the human others (i.e., non-Western peoples) became symbols for comprehending what was denied as a valid part of the self. Thus, the symbols or myths of the human others acquired significance within the Western tradition to conceptualize the untrue self, linking the human characteristics not connected with god to the human others. I will show in the next chapter that, for the West, the human other is necessary not only to define, by contrast, the West; it also serves an important mythological function in providing a more complete conceptual package in defining humankind as a whole—the whole self.

The Mythology of the Ethnic Self

People everywhere contrast themselves or their groups with other individuals or groups by means of real or imagined distinguishing characteristics. Groupness is often perpetuated through the adoption of principles such as endogamy and territoriality. When cultural features such as religious or political symbols are used to conceptualize and dramatize the boundary of the group, we use the term "ethnic" or the binomial terms "ethnic identity" or "ethnic self." Ethnic myths often deal with group origins, group superiority, and so on, and the emic discourse on these myths may be called the mythology of the ethnic self. Ethnic boundaries are maintained in relation to or in the context of interaction rather than in isolation. The contrast made between us vs. the other appears to be universal; the "us" is the people, the other the non-people.

The West, in its economic and political expansion into non-European territories, began to make a contrast between the West and the non-West; but this contrast had connotations other than those generally associated with cultural traditions in which people seek to maintain their distinctiveness vis-a-vis other groups. The non-Western groups, or human others, functioned as part of the knowledge about humankind which was necessary to provide a contrast, a representation of the non-self, to distinguish characteristics of the Western self.

The term ethnicity is often used to identify conceptions of peoplehood. I shall define ethnicity as a conglomeration of religious and political symbols used in the boundary-maintenance of cultural heritages with which people are existentially involved as a group. These symbols are often self-consciously used to construct or conceptualize ethnic identity systems. The systems themselves are distinguished by traits such as physical features, language, dress and food customs, specific religious rituals, political territory, and so on. (See Pandian 1982, particularly the introduction; also see Pandian 1977, 1978, 1981 and 1983a.)

All cultures possess symbols related to boundary-maintenance, and all humans, to a lesser or greater extent, participate in the conception or construction of ethnic identity systems; but among certain groups the active, self-conscious formulation of ethnic identity is more visible. These groups often provide an excellent laboratory for the study of ethnicity or ethnic identity systems. It is to these people with their explicit formulations of ethnic identity that scholars have usually given the term ethnic group.

Ethnicity, in terms of symbols which connote cultural boundary, is a cultural universal; but the symbols vary in content, and different types of ethnic identity systems may be identified. To associate ethnicity with minority status in sovereign political states is erroneous. In such states the dominant group often functions as the standard for what is considered desirable in physical appearance and in such areas as religion, language, food, and clothing. In such a context, the dominant group's characteristics are considered "natural," in contrast with which the characteristics of the minority group are considered "ethnic." Both, however, are equally "natural": both are cultural creations of boundedness.

Most social scientists, until recently, tended to view ethnicity as an orientation of unsophisticated, primitive thought and sentiment which stood in the way of the emergence of political modernization and civil society. Few analyzed ethnicity as a distinctive type of cultural phenomenon; the study of ethnicity was subsumed under the study of religion or politics. As George De Vos (1975:7-8) points out: "Social science theorists have until recently paid little attention to enduring ethnic or cultural identity as a primary social force comparable to nationalism or class affiliation."

Recently, however, the pendulum has reversed its swing: social science has rediscovered the importance of ethnicity. Abner Cohen (1974:1) notes: "Scholars are now 'rediscovering' in modern society the existence and significance of an endless array of patterns of symbolic behavior that have been long associated exclusively with 'primitive' society." As J.D. Gupta (1975:467) aptly puts it, "Suddenly in the sixties, the explosive demonstration of ethnic politics in the very home of mature modernity shocked those theorists into the recognition that the salience of ethnic action can hardly be inferred from the standard aggregate indices of modernity."

Since the 16th century, the Western tradition deployed a system of claiming and incorporating the lands of non-Western peoples in places such as the New World, South Africa, Australia and New Zealand, and introduced a system of colonizing countries in Asia and Africa by *explaining* why it was a moral and religious necessity. These explanations were derived from the religious and political symbols of boundary maintenance of the Western tradition, and various ethnic identity systems were constructed in order to legitimize the political dominance and boundary of the West in relation to the non-West.

In order to examine the above process, I shall refer to the studies on ethnicity by Fredrick Barth (1969) and George De Vos (1975). Barth (1969:15) suggests that the conceptualization of "the ethnic boundary" needs to be studied rather than "the cultural stuff it encloses." Likewise, De Vos (1975:6) states that it is necessary to study "how and why boundaries are maintained, rather than the cultural context of the separate group." De Vos suggests that "boundaries are basically psychological in nature, not territorial," and Barth focuses upon the "structuring of interaction which allows for the persistence of cultural differences."

The perspectives of Barth and De Vos have great merit in showing that ethnic distinctiveness is not a function of cultural, biological, or ecological isolation. However, because they minimize the analysis of "the cultural stuff or content," they neglect the importance of the meaning of historically generated symbols, their origins, elaborations and use. These symbols facilitate certain conceptualizations of group heritage, which in turn serve as orientations for certain types or kinds of ethnic identity systems of boundary-maintenance.

The type of ethnic identity system that was formulated by the West in its encounter with the non-West derived from the Judeo-Christian symbols of divinity. In the conception of Western ethnic identity, non-Western peoples were conceptualized as an aspect of the undesirable attributes of Western humanity. What was desirable, good and true derived contextual validation from the non-West, which represented the undesirable, the bad, the untrue. The Western ethnic identity system which connoted the West as morally, spiritually, intellectually and biologically superior was defined in relation to the knowledge about non-Western peoples that was incorporated in the Western tradition, knowledge that defined them as morally, spiritually, intellectually and biologically inferior.

Acculturation

The concept of acculturation commonly refers to the processes of change generated in the context of contact between peoples of different cultural traditions. The concept came into anthropological usage in the late nineteenth century, but no general consensus has yet been reached as to factors which it identifies. Ralph Beals (1953), in his review article on acculturation, shows that in spite of the fact that the concept refers to a process, it is common to speak of "degrees of acculturation" and of "partially or wholly acculturated" individuals, as if acculturation were a state of being.

A common feature in the contact between dominant and subordinate groups is that the subordinate group may discard some of its customs for those of the dominant group, and in some instances contacts can destabilize the cultural integrity of the subordinate group.

Most studies on acculturation have dealt with how or to what extent non-Western people get assimilated into the Western tradition (a process called Westernization), or have focused on the study of the non-Western reactions to the contact situation. Reactive processes include the emergence of nativistic, messianic, reformist, syncretic movements that often follow a pattern described by Anthony Wallace (1956) in his study of revitalization movements. In many contact situations cultural stress occurs, which often leads to cultural disorientation. In such contexts a prophet may emerge and promise the people a new way, or a new cultural whole. If she/he collects disciples and followers, the people may organize themselves and attempt to establish a new, viable culture. In some instances a new cultural tradition is established. Dozens of such movements have been studied by anthropologists: the Ghost Dance Movement among the Plains Indians, the Peyote

Movement among the Pueblo Indians, the Handsome Lake Movement among the Iroquois Indians, the Cargo Cult Movements in Oceania, the Prophetic Movements in Africa, and so on.

No cultural tradition has existed or exists in isolation. Contact between peoples of different cultural traditions was widespread with the expansion of the Western tradition, but contacts and borrowings have occurred ever since peripatetic *Homo sapiens* emerged as a viable biological entity. The West borrowed extensively from the non-West during Greek times and earlier, and continues to borrow, as Ralph Linton's article called "One Hundred Percent American" (1937) so humorously demonstrates. In the modern world, Western technology and other aspects of the Western tradition are borrowed extensively, in exchange for carved ancestral masks, batik and philosophies of soul-awakening and sexual postures.

And yet, throughout a human history fraught with continuous contacts and borrowings, cultural traditions promote the maintenance of their distinctiveness through the use of highly evocative religious and political symbols, symbols which have often driven people to die and kill for what they believe to be "their country," "their race," "their religion" and "their language."

Part II
Inventing the Human Other

In the statement on inventing human nature (Part I), I said that a significant area of contemporary anthropology deals with inventing human nature through the study of the cultural inventions of human nature. In the development of modern anthropology from the late Renaissance up until the turn of this century, Western cultural inventions of human nature emphasized utilitarianism and rationality as the primary foundations of human behavior and progress in order to explain the politico-economic hegemony of the West. Recent developments in anthropology (discussed earlier) have introduced a shift in the contrast which is made between the West and the non-West: both the Western and the non-Western traditions are viewed as incorporating the rational-utilitarian as well as the nonrational-symbolic aspects of human nature, but anthropology has continued to use the human other to contrast Western and non-Western cultures in terms of the knower and the known, or the studier and the studied, and to theorize about the nature of humankind.

In the next four chapters I discuss why and how the human others, i.e., peoples other than those who are considered part of the West, are integrated in the conception(s) of humankind within the Western tradition. As I mentioned in the introduction, the uniqueness of anthropology as a discipline, in my view, is in its using data on human others in combination with a non-theological perspective on humankind. I have also argued that, at the epistemological level, the above orientation of incorporating the human others is related to the Judeo-Christian orientation of dichotomizing the self, an aspect of the Western tradition which I discuss in the next chapter. In the three chapters that follow, I discuss why and how the native Americans, native Africans and other non-Western peoples were represented in a certain manner and used for conception(s) of the nature of humankind.

I use the phrase *inventing the human other* to mean the creation of the composite imageries of other people to meet emotional, intellectual and material needs of the Western tradition. These imageries acquired and acquire the significance of symbols that, in turn, were and are used to conceptualize the contrast between the West and the non-West and to theorize about the nature of humankind. I suggest in the next chapter that the imageries of fictitious, abnormal, half-human creatures that prevailed during the Medieval Period were part of the conceptualization processes of the human other in the sense that the human characteristics excluded from the conceptualization of the true self (such as cannibalism, blood-thirsty violence and greed) were attributed to the half-human beings who thus served as representations of the untrue self.

Contemporary anthropology continues to invent other peoples to serve as vehicles to conceptualize important social and intellectual problems of the Western human self today. We have invented the Yanomamo of South America as a symbol to conceptualize human aggression and sexuality. Margaret Mead invented a particular type of Samoan, Derek Freeman another; Robert Redfield and Oscar Lewis each invented a different Tepotzlan. I discuss these and other symbols in Chapter Nine. The main point to be made here is that these inventions are the result of anthropology's efforts to resolve social, intellectual and theoretical concerns and anxieties of the Western tradition.

Chapter Five

The Mythology of the Abnormal
Human Other in the Western Tradition

> And God said, "Let us make man in our image
> after our likeness." (Genesis 1: 26)
>
> And the Lord God said, "Behold the man is become
> as one of us." (Genesis 3: 22)

The Judeo-Christian Dichotomy of the Self

All societies, because of their historically evolved patterns of behavior, and the need for political and social control, make it impossible for their members to express all possible forms of human behavior. In no society, for example, is it possible for the members to engage in all forms of imagined sexuality. How, then, do societies cope with the contrast between human conduct and human possibility? An important function of religious systems is to offer various models which express the range of human possibilities, to cope with and help resolve the paradoxes of sickness and health, good and evil, life and death. Many religious systems do this through mythical representations in which the religious figures combine in their personae contradictory extremes: they are at the same time good and evil, sexual and puritanical, wild and gentle, life-giving and death-giving. For example, in Hinduism the god Siva is aptly described by Wendy O'Flaherty (1973) as an "erotic ascetic," for he is, at the same time, a symbol of expressive sexuality and repressed sexuality, self-abandonment and total self-denial.

Such mythical representations serve to provide the members of a society with symbols that aid in comprehending the consequences of extremes. Like a good play or a good novel, they make it possible for humans to comprehend the complexities of the human condition and the self; they render in concrete imagery a vision of culturally accepted truth about reality, as if to say: this is what life is.

Not all religious systems are the same in representing the arc of human possibilities. Some religious systems present mythical figures which are limited or restricted in the scope of human possibilities which they represent. They communicate a dichotomy of absolute goodness and evil, absolute strength and weakness, absolute truth and absolute untruth. The true self corresponds to goodness, strength, truth, etc. Those religions which represent their god as only good, pure, righteous, etc., have provided an absolutist statement of the nature of the human condition; they have cast out demons into the netherworld of other peoples, people who do not look like them or people whose customs are different.

The Christian God provides such a model of absolutism. He is asexual, perfect, holy. Although some psychoanalytically oriented structuralists such as Edmund Leach (1972) have suggested that the "Father" in the Christian trinity is a representation of a virile god and the "Son" is a representation of a mediating, asexual god, to the Christian believer God is a representation of the perfect, orderly, untainted primal cause. And because man is believed to be made in the image of God, this religious belief dichotomizes the conception of the self, identifies the true aspect of the self as defined for the Christian, and separates this true self from an enormous wealth of otherness in the arc of human possibilities.

In the development of the Judeo-Christian orientation, the formulation of the restrictive image of the divine being, in particular a divine being that was believed to be historical, created an absolutist, anemic mythical formula by which the West interpreted the nature of the true self. From the rich cafeteria of life, the West, beginning with the establishment of Christianity as a religio-political order, chose a rigid diet of goodness. As Tuchman (1979:32) notes, "Christianity was the matrix of medieval life.... It governed birth, marriage, and death, sex and eating, made the rules for law and medicine, gave philosophy and scholarship their subject matter." Into all aspects of life Christianity injected its dialectic between the true self and untrue self, an ongoing dance of opposites which required mediating factors. As scholarship was beginning to be secularized with the humanistic revival of learning, anthropology became the vehicle for such mediations.

The Judeo-Christian orientation contrasts sin and virtue, grace and non-grace, fall and redemption in order to comprehend the role of the divine in sustaining goodness, virtue, and so on. Within the general schema of Judeo-Christian thought it is necessary to have diametrically opposed contrasts; and within the lives of individuals, a person judges the virtuousness of his present life, achieved through the grace of God, with his sinful past.

To quote Hayden White (1972:2):

> ...the apostle Paul opposes heresy to orthodoxy (or division to unity) as the undesirable condition of the Christian community, but in such a way as to make the undesirable condition subserve the needs of the desirable one. Thus he writes: "There must be also heresies among you, that

they which are approved may be made manifest among you" (1 Cor. 11: 19).... Just as in his own *Confessions,* Augustine found it necessary to dwell upon the phenomena of sin in order to disclose the noumenal workings of grace, so too in his "prophetic history" of mankind he was compelled to focus on the sinful, heretical, insane, and damned in order to limn the area of virtue occupied by the pure, the orthodox, the sane, and the elect. Like the Puritans who came after him, Augustine found that one way of establishing the "meaning" of his own life was to deny meaning to anything radically different from it, except as antitype or negative instance.

Elaine Pagels (1981) in her book *The Gnostic Gospels* shows that there were major differences in the conception of the divine being in the history of early Christian churches. She writes:

Orthodox Jews and Christians insist that a chasm separates humanity from its creator: God is wholly other. But some of the gnostics who wrote these [gnostic] gospels contradict this: self-knowledge is knowledge of God; the self and the divine are identical.

Pagels also notes (1981:172-173):

Gnostics came to the conviction that the only way out of suffering was to realize the truth about humanity's place and destiny in the Universe. Convinced that the only answers were to be found within, the gnostic engaged on an intensely private interior journey.

Realizing the essential Self, the divine within the gnostic laughed in joy at being released from external constraints to celebrate his identification with the divine being.

But in the Judeo-Christian orientation which got established in the West from the 4th century A.D., the relationship of the self to the divinity was established through a conception of the true self because the divine being was represented as revealing truth through the faithful, the true believers, in the lineal, progressive unfolding of divine will in history. This is a theological continuation of the Hebrew tradition in which the divine being, although "lord of the universe," has a special relationship with the chosen people; and in which the principle of human meaning is derived from the knowledge of the divine being, as revealed through Hebrew history. As Huston Smith (1958:255) observes, "From the beginning to the end the Jewish quest for meaning was rooted in their understanding of God." The Christian was required to repent his sins, and reject the untrue self and knowledge of the past in order to gain the true self and knowledge.

During the Middle Ages, the myths of the Greeks lost their mythological function. No longer did they provide a text by which the West could assess the meaning of human existence. The unusual representations which had once been part of a conceptual package of the vast range of human possibility and self identity were now excluded from the restrictive mythical representation of the Judeo-Christian orientation. They became part of the general category of the untrue self which was used to define, by contrast, the true self. The untrue self was linked with the Greek myths and legends of the abnormal "wild men" that constituted a repository for those aspects of human possibility which had been excluded from an accepted definition of the true self.

Stated differently, during medieval times, the limited conceptualization of the true self with reference to the divine being resulted in the development of a category of the untrue self in association with the repository of the abnormal other into which were put unacceptable vices and desires along with images of mythical monsters and other fictional creations (such as the "wild man" believed to roam through medieval Europe on the outskirts of civilization).

During the late Renaissance, this repository of the abnormal other incorporated the non-Christian, non-Western human others and such an incorporation marked the beginning of modern anthropology. In other words, from the late Renaissance, the symbol of the abnormal other signified the non-Western, human other and connoted aspects of the untrue self.

The Fascination with the Abnormal

Humans everywhere are curious about diversity in human expression. Whether through informal gossip about the strange habits of their neighbors or through formal "teratological" studies (the science of monstrosities or abnormalities in animals and plants), all people have collected knowledge about the unusual. But the significance of these data varies; societies put this knowledge to different uses. This book considers the question of how the West came to exclude such data from an acceptable formulation of the self, dichotomizing the self into true and untrue components.

The classical Greeks and Romans were encyclopaedic in their pursuit of information, both factual and fictional. They wrote about half-human, half-animal monsters who lived in remote regions beyond the geographical limits of territories known to them. At the ends of the earth, or the "antipodes," they said, lived humans with legs on their shoulders and other aspects of their anatomy reversed. And of course they created a rich mythology in which a pantheon of divine and semi-divine beings with abnormal features cavorted through numerous human situations.

The Greeks and Romans were also aware of and had contacts with actual peoples of India and sub-Saharan Africa. In the industrious recordings of historians and naturalists such as Herodotus of the 5th century B.C. and Pliny the Elder of the 1st century A.D., ethnographic descriptions of real peoples and rumors of monstrous antipodal men were combined indiscriminately, to such an extent that modern scholars find it difficult to use their records for factual historical data (Hodgen 1964).

What did such information mean to the ancient Greeks and Romans? It is important to distinguish two uses of information on the unusual. 1) The Greeks developed a rich mythology in which they allowed their imaginations full play in expressing the range of human possibilities. The mythical representations constituted a divine charter for the Greeks, a definition of what was acceptable in the self. The unusual images of divine beings and monsters were not, in this sense, aspects of the untrue self; they promoted an awareness and acceptance of the unusual within the range of human possibility. The divine stage was a human stage, a metaphorical representation of the complexity of human reality which embraced paradoxical extremes. 2) At the same time, the Greeks, like all peoples, distinguished Greekness from non-Greekness. The actual peoples they encountered in India and Africa were assigned to the category of non-people. But this otherness was not imbued with significance. The myths of the Greeks satisfied the need, universal in humans, to develop a meaning system that dealt with the diversity and integrity of the self. Their myths, because they were complex representations that dramatized several human possibilities, made myths of the human other unnecessary. The human other may or may not have been unusual — sometimes similarities in customs were noted, sometimes differences — but his unusualness did not take on significance to represent the diversity of human expression; the knowledge of diversity and complexity was already provided by Greek myths. The human other was irrelevant to the Greeks; the writings of Herodotus did not serve as a model to comprehend the nature of humankind; they served no mythological function.

To Christian Europe of the Middle Ages, the abnormal other was, as to the Greeks, a source of interest and amusement; and also like the Greeks, medieval Europeans did not see the abnormal other as having significance, as being something to which one could go for an understanding of humanity as a whole. As Saint Augustine declared, God revealed truth in history through the faithful; in writing the universal history, the non-Christians were included as the non-significant others who did not have the truth. The abnormal other was a repertoire of vices, and could be used as a contrasting category to conceptualize the dichotomy between the true self and the untrue self. But there was no need to study or incorporate the abnormal other to understand humanity; humanity was comprehended through the true self linked with the divine being.

Only during the late Renaissance did Europe's history of fascination with the abnormal other merge with newly discovered non-Western human others. The abnormal/non-Western other served as symbolic representations for conceptualizing the self as a whole, incorporating the true self as the knower or signifier and the untrue self as an aspect to be known for an understanding of humanity as a whole.

In other words, for the West since the late Renaissance, the human other is necessary not only to define, by contrast, the West; it also serves important mythological functions in providing a more complete conceptual package in defining humankind as a whole — the whole self. As the Western tradition has excluded many possibilities in its construction of a definition of the true self, and projects these excluded possibilities onto the human other in order to understand the undichotomized self, the West uses the symbols of divinity and those of the human other to achieve a complete understanding of what it means to be human. In this sense, anthropology, along with other Western disciplines (such as the so-called "depth psychologies" of Freud, Jung and others), serve mythological functions of incorporating the untrue self or the human other to cope with the human condition.

The anthropologist, with his museums and artifacts, material and nonmaterial, is a modern rendition of the West's preoccupation with descriptions and classifications of unusual beings, customs and practices, which since the Renaissance have served to flesh out the construct of the human other. Textbooks in anthropology compete in their choice of unusual pictures and descriptions of the rituals and practices of the non-Western peoples, customs which, from the Western cultural perspective, are thought of as abnormal, not a valid model for the true self. Although modern anthropology rejects the concept of "abnormal customs" and has replaced words such as "bizarre" and "exotic" with other words such as "different" or "distinctive," the former was commonly used at an earlier time (and even today an occasional irreverent anthropologist will describe her/his profession as the "study of the queer and the quaint"). The Pango Pango Principle still operates, however: the more bizarre the custom — the more unusual the mortuary rite, the more distinctive the sexual practice, the more detailed the description of the clitoridectomy — then the more useful is this example of human otherness in shedding light on human nature.

Chapter Six

The Mythology of the Fossil Human Other in the Western Tradition

The Fossil Other in the Judeo-Christian
Lineal Conception of History

Fossil (Random House Dictionary 1966): any remains, impression or trace of an animal or plant of a former geological age...an out-dated or old-fashioned person or thing...belonging to a past epoch or discarded system; fossilized; antiquated...derives from the Latin *fossil(is)*, dug up.

We have discussed the mythology of the human other in the Western tradition, and the dichotomy of the self into true and untrue components. Different scholars have tried various ways of distinguishing between the human other and us and achieving a synthesis of these true and untrue components, distinguishing the irrational past from the rational present (the myth of the savage other), the lack of mental development of the other with the progress of the Western mind (the myth of the black other), and the ahistorical human other with the historical us (the myth of the ethnographic other). These versions of the myth of the human other will be discussed in Chapters Seven, Eight and Nine. In this chapter, however, I will discuss concepts such as psychic unity, progress and unitormitarianism which pertain to the identification of the human other as a fossil.

The Judeo-Christian lineal conception of history relegates the untrue self to the past. The human other represents ourselves as we were before knowledge. Within the Christian conception of universal history it was unnecessary to study the human other; the human other served as a contrast to comprehend knowledge as it was revealed to Christians. But, beginning with the Renaissance, when humanistic learning became acceptable, the study of human others to excavate past strata of the self became prevalent. (This excavation has become steadily interiorized, as I suggest in the final section of this chapter, so that today we are excavating not only the archaeological sites of primeval man but also the unconscious of the human mind.)

The connotations of the symbol "fossil" (belonging to an earlier age, an original form; an antiquated, outmoded form which has been superseded by modern forms) have received differing emphases as the West, over several centuries, used it to discuss human others. From a concern with defining the original state of human nature, the West shifted to an emphasis on the outmoded character of original forms. In this sense the symbol of the fossil other was used to conceptualize the changing, dynamic West in contrast with the static, non-changing, fossilized, non-Western peoples.

Ever since classical antiquity, scholars have tried to understand the "original" state of human nature in the sense of what was primeval/primary/primitive, and what was natural. Lovejoy et al. (1935), documenting the history of the ideas of primitivism and naturalness, distinguish two philosophies of primitivism in Greek thought: 1) "chronological primitivism" was a philosophy of history in which ancient or early periods of human history were considered glorious times. Man led a simple and unfettered life. When man founded complex institutions, the simple purity of early life degenerated or decayed. 2) "Cultural primitivism" extolled the virtues of the simple life without postulating that the historical beginnings of humankind were rooted in the simple life. The concept of naturalness (Lovejoy and his associates identify sixty-six different meanings of the words "natural" and "nature") also connoted an ideal state of being.

Thus in Greek thought, certain forms of human expression could be examined for what they revealed about the original, natural state of mind or society. But only during the Renaissance were non-Western peoples perceived as the embodiment of primitive man and the natural man. After that, depending on the needs of Western society, the connotations of fossildom received different emphasis. Were non-Western peoples (as fossil others) natural men representing noble innocence or the primeval West? Or were they anomalous relics, "living fossils" out of tune with the changing times, superseded by the progressive dynamism of the West? In the late 19th century, the latter meaning was expanded and strengthened with the development of the social Darwinism which idealized individualism and the notion of the survival of the fittest.

The Fossil Other in the Late Renaissance and the Enlightenment

By the late 17th century the concept of progress became important and the West was conceptualized as having progressed; non-Western societies were compared with temporally ancient, extinct societies as having not progressed. The human other was perceived as a living fossil, a contemporary representation of the West's own past; he was static, fixed in time. Non-Western traditions were, in effect, used as a synchronic model to explain diachronic developments in the Western tradition.

The use of data on non-Western traditions to derive an understanding of the original state of humankind required the assumption of psychic unity, that those who have not progressed are the "same" in some ways as those who have progressed; they were the fossils of ourselves. In the 18th century's emphasis on a mechanistic universe and the operation of natural laws, achievement in the sciences was the mark of progress, and education was the route to progress. With education and training in reason, all humans could progress. That the mind operated everywhere, or that there was uniformity in the laws of the human mind, was a law of nature. A law could not be a law, by the canons of reason, unless it operated in a uniform manner.

Progress, then, had several different meanings in the 17th and 18th centuries. The Enlightenment focused on the advancements in science as the result of improved education and exercise in reason. The human mind obeyed the same laws; through understanding these natural laws and applying this knowledge, all peoples could progress.

The Fossil Other in the 19th Century

The egalitarian, utilitarian models of the Enlightenment were undermined in the early 19th century when the theological and Romantic models became popular. Burrow (1966) discusses modifications in the concept of psychic unity which occurred in response to social-political trends. From assumed uniformity, the mind became stratified; non-Western peoples were not only seen as living fossils of the primeval West, but they became archaic, stunted, undeveloped forms. Although the origins of this shift in conception of the fossil other stemmed from colonialism, the language was couched in the terms of biological evolution. History became biologized, and the era of scientific racism began (Harris 1968).

By the mid-19th century, most non-Western societies were under the economic and political domination of the West. Concomitant with this inequality in power arose assumptions about unequal distribution of intellectual endowments. The explanatory model for these differences was no longer couched in the mechanistic worldview of the Enlightenment, in which it was assumed that the laws of reason were everywhere the same and differences in custom were the result of the improper use of reason caused by the influence of experience, environment and education. In this mechanistic worldview, mind was an entity, a machine, a uniform system on which mechanistic influences such as education operated to speed it up or slow it down.

But in the 19th century, the mechanistic worldview had changed to a biological worldview, and the notion of the fossil other acquired biological

connotations. The West was civilized because the Western mind had
evolved biologically. The non-Western mind had not evolved; it was at a
primitive, undeveloped stage, a form which had not survived the tests of
time and thus was less fit to survive than was the Western tradition.

From about the middle of the 19th century, great advances were made in
geology and biology. From geology came the principle of uniformitarianism, or the doctrine of uniform causes, the idea that the geological processes which operated in the past to create the geological strata observable
today are the same processes which can be seen operating in the present.
This concept is probably a continuation of the mechanistic worldview of the
Enlightenment, but it also supported the developments in biology, allowing
people to conceptualize the deposits of archaic fossils in lower strata; it may
even have conveyed or supported the image of stratified mental development which developed during this time. It enabled people to imagine the
idea of different peoples becoming fossilized, or frozen in time, at
particular strata or layers of progressive evolution.

Geology developed in conjunction with evolutionary biology,
stratigraphy and the principle of uniformitarianism serving to expand the
period of time since the earth was created, providing eons for evolution (or
biological "progress") to occur. The ancient remains of extinct forms
found in geological strata were related to living forms; genetic relationships
were established among all living organisms. Questions were asked about
why some forms had survived while others did not; the biological answers
were phrased in such terms as "survival of the fittest," and "struggle for
existence." The philosophy of "Social Darwinism," which was not a byproduct of Darwinian constructs at all but was part of the general worldview of the time, made perfect sense in this context, and served to justify
colonialism and the domination of non-Western peoples.

The biological model was applied to explain differences in human customs and institutions. Just as some biological organisms could be termed
"survivals" or "living fossils" because they were almost identical to primitive forms found buried in earlier strata, so non-Western primitive societies
could also be thought of as representing earlier stages of phylogenetic development.

But what was it that progressed, or evolved, in human societies? In the
18th century all peoples were believed to have the "same" mind on which
experiences operated; but in the 19th century different stages of human
mental development were distinguished. Each stage was characterized by
similar or uniform mental structures, with each stage producing different
customs. The West had progressed through earlier stages but was now at the
peak of human mental development. Although non-Western peoples had
the capacity to progress and attain the same level as the West, they were
now like "children," and should be treated as such. The Haeckelian notion
of "ontogeny recapitulates phylogeny," i.e., the idea that individual organ-

isms exhibit in their development the developmental stages of the phylum, became popular. The adult human other was like the child of the Western tradition; Western children behaved like non-Western adults and in their adult stage were different from the adult human other. Thus, while the principle of psychic unity was not rejected, a stratified model of mental capacity was affirmed, and non-Western peoples were considered to be at lower, less developed stages of mental development.

Scholars of the 19th century were preoccupied with writing the "natural history of the mind," in which the mind was seen to manifest different types of institutions at varying stages of development. In Germany scholars such as Hegel traced the evolution or progress of the mind as spirit, or as idea becoming progressively aware of itself. The West, and Germany in particular, had attained the fullest awareness; in it, the spirit had unfolded, evolved. In most non-Western societies, however, the spirit was less aware, less evolved. (Levi-Strauss has reversed Hegel, locating rationality in the non-Western other; but in the process of denying progress of mind, he also denies historicity to the human other.)

Anthropology, which was professionalized in the 19th century, explained customs with reference to stages of human development, or "culture." Edward Tylor (often identified as the "father of anthropology") and Louis Henry Morgan (the American lawyer turned anthropologist, often identified as the "father of kinship studies") demonstrated that there were different stages of cultural development, and that similar institutions existed in correspondence to different stages of mental development. Museums were organized not to portray the "cultures" of particular peoples, but to demonstrate levels of cultural development. For example, weaponry from societies all over the world might be grouped together to demonstrate the level of "savagery," in contrast with "barbarism" or "civilization," the latter, of course, representing the apex of cultural progress.

For other anthropologists, the alignment of non-Western others in a stratified model of mind or culture took on a more biological character. In general, late 19th-century anthropology constituted what Marvin Harris (1968) calls "biologized history" in that institutions were not only placed at lower or higher levels in relation to lower or higher mental development, but they were also interpreted as expressions of different biogenetic endowments. Not only were the anthropological comparisons of the 19th century "natural histories of the mind," they were also "racial-cultural histories of mankind," and a fallacious link was forged between language, race and culture. The stratified grouping of peoples according to physical variations had occurred since the 15th century and was related to the institution of slavery, but now the Darwinian model provided an explanation for the differences in which they already believed. Scientific racism is still alive and well in the 20th century. (See Chapter Eight.)

With the biologizing of the fossil other, what happened to the concept of psychic unity? The following quote from Stocking (1968: 115-116) gives a fairly accurate assessment of the concept as it came to be understood by the late 19th century:

> Of the three major Victorian evolutionists...E.B. Tylor is the one who departed least from the 18th century model in his thinking on the psychic unity of man....But there is other evidence to suggest that Tylor regarded, or came to regard, the mental evolution of savage to civilized man as structural as well as functional....he suggested in 1881 that these showed "a connexion between a more full and intricate system of brain-cells and fibres, and a higher intellectual power, in the races which have risen in the scale of civilization." Tylor went on to say that the "history of civilization teaches, that up to a certain point savages and barbarians are like what our ancestors were and our peasants still are, but from this level the superior intellect of the progressive races has raised their nations to heights of culture." It is not clear whether Tylor felt that these mental differences were cause or consequences of a higher civilization; in either case they are an important qualification of the 18th century view of psychic unity.

The evolutionary model in terms of which the fossil other was defined and interpreted was, by the 20th century, challenged on all fronts, and the comparative method of evolutionary anthropology was challenged. The biological model remains significant, however, in the Western conception of the black other (See Chapter Eight).

Exteriorization and Interiorization of the Other

Hayden White (1972) notes that there has been a progressive interiorization of the "wild man," the "savage," and the "primitive" in anthropology. What was once conceptualized as the referent for the untrue self, the qualities that were exteriorized, are now interiorized or internalized. Thus anthropology promotes the view that the wild man is in us also. Both the divine being and the human other have external referents but are made internal to recognize and accept the true self and the untrue self.

The mythology of the fossil other is still with us today but has also become internalized. No longer is the fossil other a temporal concept but a structural principle. To discover the fossil other we must, according to Levi-Strauss, excavate the mind of the human other; the fossil is in us also, but is buried much too deep, like the Jungian archetypes of our unconscious. But just as it is necessary to understand both the true and the untrue self to get a full understanding of the self, so one must understand both the conscious and unconscious to understand the mind.

Modern anthropologists frequently suggest that we should understand ourselves by understanding the nature of human others, that we should learn to see other cultures in ourselves. The human other is in us, and we are in human others. Anthropology's preoccupation with the human other has produced various rationalizations concerning the *need* to study, to objectify, to salvage in print the cultures of other peoples. Human others are seen as homologous and analogous to our own ancestors, and an understanding of the human other is considered necessary to enable us to unravel human origins, to learn about the early cultures of the West and also our own unconscious. Our past, the dead past, is in the human other's living present. This other has no history; this other is the eternal present, the "ethnographic present" (see Chapter Nine).

What are the social
Functions + historical
sources of the Savg +
Black other in W. Trad.

Chapter Seven

The Mythology of the Savage
Other in the Western Tradition

The Locus of the Symbol of the Savage Other

The savage other was an abnormal other, but with distinctive characteristics which derived from myths of primordial man and legends of wild
men, and came to incorporate as its specific referents the data on American
Indians and sub-Saharan Africans. The savage other (specifically represented by Indians and Africans) came to stand for the antithesis of the rational and orderly us; the savage was the epitome of irrationality and disorder.

Hayden White (1972:4) points out that

> The notion of "wildness" (or in its Latinate form, "savagery") belongs
> to a set of culturally self-authenticating devices which includes, among
> others, the ideas of "madness" and "heresy" as well. These terms are
> used not merely to designate a specific condition or state of being but
> also to confirm the value of their dialectical antithesis: "civilization,"
> "sanity," and "orthodoxy" as well.

The Random House Dictionary (1966) defines savage in the following
ways:

> fierce, ferocious, or cruel; untamed...uncivilized; barbarous...en-
> raged or furiously angry...unpolished, rude...wild or rugged...un-
> cultivated; growing wild...an uncivilized human being...a fierce,
> brutal, or cruel person...a rude, boorish person.

The word is derived from Latin *silv(a)*, woods, a derivation similar to that
of "heathen," which according to Taylor (1925:169-170) comes from an
Anglo-Saxon word denoting dwellers of heath or country. Such denotations
came to connote a contrast between the pagan, uncivilized country and the
Christian, orderly *civitas*.

The word savagery acquired different meanings in English, French and

62

German. The term is ambiguous, as the above range of definitions indicate, implying simplicity of uncivilized or uncultured life, and at the same time representing the brutal ferocity of animals. The savage is outside of order, outside of society, non-Christian, a woodland being who is hypersexed and endowed with super-normal physical powers. The savage is a cannibal, half beast and half human.

In the use of the concept of the savage, the meanings given to it shifted, depending on a particular country's orientation toward the human other, and the speaker's projection of positive or negative attributes of humanity onto this other. The savage could be noble or ignoble. The essence of being a savage was the lack of order or constraints. If the lack of constraints was considered good, then the image of the savage produced positive responses. If lack of constraints was considered destructive, then the image of savage produced fear of the human other.

The half-beast/half-human imagery of the savage acquired a complex set of attributes during the Middle Ages. During this time the concept of the symbol of savage had concrete references in the "wild man" who was believed to live in the forests of Europe. Richard Bernheimer, in *Wild Men in the Middle Ages* (1952), discusses how the psychological needs of the people of the Middle Ages were met by the symbol of the wild man. The wild man was an ambiguous, anomalous monster who did not fit in the classificatory categories of the Great Chain of Being. He was excessively sexual, lurking in the woods where he waited to seize, carry off and defile civilized women, and to devour innocent babes. Living at the edge of civilization as a naked, hairy beast, he was himself emotionally involved in the life of civilized humans.

Bernheimer asks why this imagery existed in the Middle Ages and concludes:

> It appears that the notion of the wild man must respond and be due to a persistent psychological urge. We may define this urge as the need to give external expression and symbolically valid form to the impulses of reckless physical self-assertion which are hidden in all of us, but are normally kept under control. . . . But the repressed desire for such un-hampered self-assertion persists and may finally be projected outward as the image of a man who is as free as the beasts, able and ready to try his strength without regard for the consequences to others, and there-fore able to call up forces which his civilized brother has repressed in his effort at self-control. In contrast to civilized man, the wild man is a child of nature, upon whose hidden resources he can depend, since he has not removed himself from its guidance and tutelage. (Bernheimer 1952:3-4)

Whatever the validity of these psychological assumptions, they are con-stants (all societies impose restraints on their members) and cannot be used to explain the particular cultural expression of the wild man in the West. I pointed out earlier that the West had a long tradition of describing mythical monsters and antipodal men. During the Middle Ages, such representations of human possibility were excluded from a concept of the self; they were conceived of as pagan beliefs, marginal to Christianity. Christianity came to represent order, these pagan images disorder, and the symbol of savagery took on its connotations of non-Christian chaos. However, the church had difficulty linking the idea of savagery with specific referents such as wild men because of its insistence on the principle of monogenesis. If man is the product of a single act of creation, then how are anomalous half-men to be explained? This cognitive problem was never resolved during the Middle Ages, but during the Renaissance, particularly in the 17th century when the symbol of the savage acquired a concrete reference in American Indians and sub-Saharan Africans, all these fictional and non-fictional beings were defined as sub-human and located below humans on the Great Scale of Being. The savage became a mediator, a missing link, between animal and man.

According to Hodgen (1964:417-418):

> ...in the interval between the thirteenth and seventeenth centuries, or for four hundred years after the writing of Albert's *De animalibus* [in which he classified apes as *Homo*] little was said of a philosophical or scientific nature concerning the possibility either of a semi-animal link between man and other forms lower in the hierarchy, or of the savage as a possible transitional figure. It was too remote a problem for the times....

> The Break came in the last quarter of the seventeenth century and the first third of the eighteenth with Sir William Petty's abortive essay entitled *The scale of creatures* (1676-77), Sir William Tyson's *Orangoutang, sive homo silvestris; or, the anatomy of a pygmie* (1708), and Carl Linnaeus' *System of nature* (1735). After the publication of these books mankind was no longer considered a perfect whole....In both biological and ethnological inquiry the discovery of "missing links" became the order of the day.

In some versions of the Christian origin myth, Adam and Eve are themselves portrayed as hair-hairy wildmen. The attribute of the wild man image which is being conveyed here, however, is not disorder but elemental, single primitiveness; Adam and Eve in the Garden of Eden belong to an age of innocence.

Land and Order: The Discovery of the New World

The discovery and colonization of the New World brought a tremendous shift in the European's perception of his relationship to human others. Before the discovery of the New World, Europe was familiar with the physical and cultural differences which existed among the peoples of Europe, the Muslim world, India and sub-Saharan Africa. According to the principle of monogenesis, such variations did not detract from an acceptance of the common unity of mankind; such peoples were all considered human, although some may have "degenerated."

The sale of sub-Saharan Africans as slaves began in the middle of the 15th century, before the discovery of the New World, and probably would have stopped within a few decades except for this discovery. The discovery of the New World posed an economic, political and cognitive problem for the European. Colonial expansion brought this land within the cognitive as well as the political territory of Europe. No longer were these strange other peoples located in the non-European antipodes; they were now part of European territory. What position was the European to take in this "new" world? To assume economic and political mastery, he must also claim human superiority; he became the only human, and all others were reduced to sub-human status.

The existing view of the sub-Saharan African as a degenerated form of humanity was extended (see further discussion in Chapter Eight), as a new category of sub-humans was created on the Great Chain of Being. The Africans, whose use as slaves was limited in Europe, could now be put to full use as human cattle.

The Africans, however, were not from the New World itself. They had been subdued, displaced from their own country, and posed no threat to the European quest for economic, political and cognitive domination over the New World. The American Indians, however, were the original occupants of the land; and it was with them that Europeans became preoccupied. It was not sufficient to exclude them from the human race, along with Africans; they also became embodiments of all that was non-Christian, uncivilized and disorderly. The American Indian became the concrete referent for the symbol of the savage other.

What images do we find of American Indians during this time of colonial expansion? They were portrayed as proud but wild, a powerful, dangerous antagonist to good, Christian life. Seen as blood-thirsty, cannibalistic killers, they could themselves be slaughtered without mercy. Seen as non-Christian others, the Indians did not have to be treated in a Christian manner. In the early 16th century, until the Pope declared that the Indians were fully human, the killing of Indians posed no moral dilemma for the Conquistadores. According to Haddon (1934), the Spaniards felt no compunction in slaughtering the American natives because they were not the descendents of Adam and Eve. As heathens who did not cultivate the soil, they did not deserve to keep it; the Europeans saw it as their duty to cultivate the land, to bring it under Christian influence.

The American Indian became the primary referent for the symbol of the savage other from the late Renaissance onward, for he posed the greatest threat to European dominance in the new, expanded world in which the European found himself. Depending on who described the American Indian and why, the image of the Indian varied, shifting between positive and negative attributes. (See, for example, Robert F. Berkhofer, Jr., *The White Man's Indian: Images of the American Indian from Columbus to the Present* (1978), for an excellent discussion of the role of theology and anthropology in generating and sustaining various positive and/or negative images of Indians using the symbol of the savage.)

Jennings (1975) argues that by the late 16th century, the connotation of "beastly ferocity" became the dominant meaning conveyed by the term "savage" in English, after English settlers had come into various conflicts with native Americans. The event which completed the process, for the English, of making the Indian the major ethnographic referent for the symbol of savagery was the so-called "Indian Uprising" (or, from the Indians' point of view, the "Indian Liberation Movement") of 1622. Thereafter, the images of Indians reflect this conflict. In 1624, for example, we find John Smith identifying the Indians as savages, as cruel beasts even more unnatural and brutish than beasts.

The French word *sauvage,* however, combined ideas of noble primitivism with beastiality, and continued to be an ambiguous symbol until the late 19th century, reflecting a different kind of relationship which French colonists had with the Indians. Kennedy (1950) argues that the French use of the symbol of savage became similar to the English usage only in the 19th century. Both English and French colonists had preconceived notions of the "inhuman ferocity" of the Indians from Spanish documents; but such a conception was maintained or altered, respectively, through interaction.

This linkup between ownership of land, displacement of the original owners of the land, the English development of real estate in the New World, and the political and military aspects of British settlements in the New World has been emphasized by several historians. The following quotes from the book *Red, White and Black* (Nash 1974:40-42) clearly illustrates the relationship between these factors and the fluctuation in positive and negative images of the American Indian:

> As early as the 1580's, George Peckham, an early promoter of colonization, had admitted that some Englishmen doubted their right to take possession of the land of others....
>
> To some extent the problem could be resolved by arguing that Englishmen did not intend to take the Indians' land but wanted only to share with them what seemed a superabundance of territory.... It was this argument that the governing council in Virginia used in 1610 when it advertised in England that the settlers "by way of marchandizing and trade, doe buy of them...the pearles of earth, and sell them the pearles of heaven."

The English also resolved the problem of the Indians' possession of the land by refusing to accept them as human. To continue the Nash quotation:

> "Although the Lord hath given the earth to children of men," [wrote Robert Gray in 1609] "the greater part of it [is] possessed and wrongfully usurped by wild beasts, and unreasonable creatures, or by brutish savages, which by reason of their godles ignorance, and blasphemous Idolatrie, are worse than those beasts which are of most wilde and savage nature."

The Symbol of the Savage Other
Differences between Renaissance and Enlightenment Anthropology

The authority of the Catholic Church weakened in the Renaissance, particularly during the late Renaissance, and alternative sources of authority emerged. While Protestants sought legitimacy in the authority of the Bible, secular thinkers went to the Classics. In the absence of a monolithic hierarchical structure which defined the nature of man and society, diverse interpretations were made, and the idea of polygenesis gained wider currency. As I have previously stated, the late Renaissance was a period of great learning, but also of violent conflict (later defined by Enlightenment thinkers as "irrational" activities) in the form of virulent anti-Semitism, apocalyptic beliefs, millennarianism and persecution of witches.

For reasons discussed in the previous section, thinkers of the late Renaissance saw in American Indians and Africans a concrete manifestation of the symbol of savagery with all its negative connotations. As the ideas of polygenesis became accepted—scholars now debated the multiple creations of God in particular, and the nature of God in general— the savage other (as represented by Indians and Africans) was placed on the Great Chain of Being as sub-human. Discussion of the nature of mankind and diversity of customs—the anthropology of this time—centered on where exactly the savage should be placed on the chain. Was he closer to the beasts, or was he closer to humans? Scholars were divided on the issue. Some, such as Montaigne, emphasized the diversity of customs but upheld the status of savages as humans. Others classified Africans and Indians as beasts, exhibiting them in association with beasts to show their affinity.

In the use of the symbol of the savage, one of the most common conceptual contrasts made in the 17th century was between rationality and irrationality. The identification of the savage as irrational in contrast with rational Western man received its fullest expression and development during the 18th-century Enlightenment.

Scholars of the 18th century inherited a legacy, developed in the preceding epoch, by which the diversity in customs could be explained in terms of progress and degeneration. Fontenelle in the late 17th and early 18th centuries set the stage for discussing progress in human affairs in abstract terms. Gradually, with the growth of science and the description of peoples in naturalistic terms, rationality came to be seen as the prime mover in progress. It was the marker by which Enlightenment thinkers distinguished themselves from the Renaissance, and the key by which they interpreted differences in the customs of various peoples.

During the Enlightenment, various taxonomies of human others existed. The Linnaean classification had a place for human monsters, wild men and savages. Count Buffon introduced the concept of race to discuss human variation. Blumenbach provided a classification of human races, including the category "Caucasian." The development and significance of racial symbols is discussed in Chapter Eight. What is of interest here is that during the Enlightenment, all of these human others were embraced under the principle of the psychic unity of mankind. American Indians and Africans, as concrete referents of the symbol of the savage other, were accepted as human beings. All humans, savages included, were believed to have a common mental structure; differences could be explained by whether or not people used their rational capabilities. The Medieval West had been irrational; the Enlightenment had progressed because of its focus on rationality. In a similar way, the savage others could aspire to progress, to achieve the perfect institutions of the West through education. The French statesman Anne Robert Jacques Turgot, writing in the 18th century, compared genius in humanity to the gold in a mine; the more the soil is mined, the more metal can be found. If education and opportunity are lacking, genius lies forever hidden. Turgot conceived of the study of "universal history," in which the laws governing institutions could be revealed. His definition of universal history is very similar to the contemporary conception of culture in anthropology.

The 18th century produced excellent ethnographies. The comparative method, evolved in the late Renaissance, was applied systematically. One of the foremost ethnographers and ethnologists of this period was the Jesuit priest J.F. Lafitau (1681-1746). Lafitau's two-volume work on Indians, published in 1724, was, according to William Fenton (1979:173), "the first blaze on the path to scientific anthropology." Lafitau described the religious and other customs of the Indians of his time, and compared these customs to those of classical antiquity. His comparative method was based on three major propositions: 1) as man was created by God and all humans are descended from that single act of creation, all men share common mental structures; this accounts for cultural universals; 2) the differences between societies stem from differences in climate and from separation and migration of groups; 3) the original state of society which man had at the beginning of creation—and here Lafitau was concerned with defining monotheism as the primordial religious belief—has degenerated, giving rise to differences.

Lafitau was not only an ethnologist who used the comparative method systematically, he was also an ethnographer who sought to describe Iroquois culture "in its own terms," a phrase frequently used by modern anthropologists. His work is representative of the 18th century.

The conceptual contrast between rationality and irrationality, and use of non-Western others to represent the irrationality of the savage other, continued into the next century. In the 20th century, however, there occurred a curious transformation in the symbol of the savage other. According to White (1972:7):

> ...the idea of the Wild Man was progressively despatialized. This despatialization was attended by a compensatory process of psychic interiorization. And the result has been that modern cultural anthropology has conceptualized the idea of wildness as the repressed content of *both* civilized *and* primitive humanity. So that, instead of the relatively comforting thought that the Wild Man may exist *out there* and can be contained by some kind of physical action, it is now thought... that the Wild Man is lurking within every man, is clamoring for release within us all, and will be denied only at the cost of life itself.

By the middle of the 20th century, wildness and primitive simplicity had become internalized in all humanity.

Congruent with the symbols of savagery and stasis to characterize the non-Western other, the symbol of the black other, which evolved in the 16th century, now serves to distinguish West from non-West. Unlike previous symbols of otherness, the black other has never been internalized by the West, and this is the essence of racism today. The black other — a symbol which refers not only to Africans but all non-Western peoples — is not in us.

Chapter Eight

The Mythology of the Black
Other in the Western Tradition

Classifications of Humans Based on Color
During the Renaissance and the Enlightenment

The Random House Dictionary defines "black" in the following ways:

> ...lacking hue and brightness...soiled or stained with dirt...character-
> ized by absence of light...gloomy, pessimistic, dismal...boding ill,
> sullen, hostile...deliberate, harmful, inexcusable...without any moral
> light or goodness, evil, wicked...marked by ruin or desolation...
> indicating censure, disgrace, or liability to punishment...unfinished
> (steel)...the color at the extreme end of grays, opposite to white...
> a member of a dark-skinned people; Negro.

It is beyond the scope of this book to discuss the origin of the conceptual
dichotomy between good and evil in relation to color. There is evidence that
Western civilization developed an associated set of dualisms between good
and evil, day and night, life and death, which were connected with the
colors black and white since at least the days of Heraclitus. White (1972:15)
comments on the Hebrew preoccupation with species mixture and color.
But whether this is to be interpreted as some kind of universal structural
principle or as a specific aspect of Western tradition is irrelevant to the
argument presented here. As we are concerned with the Renaissance
foundations of anthropological thought, we shall examine how the Renaissance thinkers conceived of variations in color in human beings.

As the following quotations from Slotkin (1965:passim) indicate,
Renaissance thinkers used color as one of several criteria of classification,
but the peoples they separated or joined under particular categories are
classified differently today. Of particular note is the absence of a general
category of "black" which today is used to incorporate all Africans as well
as dark-skinned peoples from other countries (and in general all non-
Western peoples), and which implies a racial archetype which has come to

connote moral, intellectual, social and medical inferiority. The term "black" was used as a descriptive term; variations in skin color among Africans and other darker-skinned populations were noted.

In his *Notebooks,* Leonardo da Vinci (1452-1519) wrote:

> The black races in Ethiopia are not the product of the sun; for if black gets black with child in Scythia, the offspring is black; but if a black gets a white woman with child the offspring is grey. And this shows that the seed of the mother has power in the embryo equally with that of the father.

Jean Bodin (1530-1596) wrote:

> ...the people of the South are of a contrarie humour and disposition to them of the North: these are great and strong, they are little and weak; they of the north hote and moyst, the others cold and dry; the one hath a big voyce and greene eyes, the other hath a weake voyce and black eyes; the one hath a flaxen haire and a faire skin, the other hath both haire and skin black; the one feareth cold, and the other heate; the one is joyfull and pleasant, the other sad; the one is fearefull and peaceable, the other is hardie and mutinous; the one is sociable, the other solitarie; the one is given to drinke, the other sober; the one rude and grosse witted, the other advised and ceremonious; the one is prodigall and greedie, the other is covetous and holds fast; the one is a souldier, the other a philosopher; the one fit for armes and labour, the other for knowledge and rest.

In the words of Isac de La Peyrere (1594-1676):

> As many Difficulties lie against the Mosaick System of confining all Species of living terrestrial Creatures within the Asiatick or Primaeval Paradise, and afterwards to Noah's Ark; so more seem to arise against the Propagation of all Mankind out of one single Male and Female, unless all Posterity, both Blacks and Whites, separated by vast Seas, were all included actually in Form within Adam and Eve.

> The Origin of Negroes lies very obscure; for Time out of Mind there hath been Blacks with a wooly Substance on their Bodies instead of Hair; because they are mentioned in the most ancient Records now extant in the World. Tis plain, their Colour and Wool are innate, or seminal from their first Beginning, and seems to be a specifick Character, which neither the Sun, nor any Curse from Cham could imprint upon them.

> Not the first, because many other Nations, living under the same Climates and Heats, are never black; as the Abyssines, the Siamites, the Brasilians, Peruvians, etc. neither will any White ever become a Black, in Guinea, Congo, or Angola, though born there; neither will any Negroes produce Whites in Virginia, or New England. The Textures of their Skins and Blood differ from those of Whites.

> Not the latter; for what Curse is Change of Colour, that being only acci-

dental to Beauty, which consists wholly in Proportion and Symmetry?
The old Statues in black Marble, are as much, if not more, valued than
those in white. Besides, the Curse upon Cham's Account must have
turn'd many of the Asiaticks, and all the Egyptians, into Negroes; for
they were curs'd more peculiarly than the western remote Coasts of
Africa.

This Colour (which appears to be as ingenite, and as original as that in
Whites) could not proceed from any Accident; because, when animals
are accidentally black, they do not procreate constantly black ones, (as
the Negroes do) as in Dogs, Cows, Sheep, and in some Birds; accidental
Colours vary in the same numerical Subject by Changes of Season, of
Diet, of Culture, etc. but a Negroe will always be a Negroe, carry him
to Greenland, give him Chalk, feed and manage him never so many
Ways.

William Petty (1623-1687) said:

Besides those differences between Man and man, there bee others more
considerable, that is, between the Guiny Negros and the Middle Europeans; and of Negros between those of Guiny and those who live about
the Cape of Good Hope, which last are the Most beastlike of all the
Souls of Men with whom our Travellers are well acquainted. I say that
the Europeans do not onely differ from the aforementioned Africans in
Colour, which is as much as white differs from black, but also in their
Haire which differs as much as a straight line differs from a Circle; but
they differ also in the shape of their Noses, Lipps and cheek bones, as
also in the very outline of their faces and the Mould of their skulls.
They differ also in their Naturall Manners, and in the internall Qualities
of their Minds.

Francois Bernier (1620-1688) also provided a classification of human
groups:

Although in the exterior form of their body, and especially in their
faces, men are almost all different one from the other, according to the
different districts of the earth which they inhabit . . . still I have remarked
that there are four or five species or races of men in particular whose
difference is so remarkable that it may be properly made use of as the
foundation for a new division of the earth.

I comprehend under the first species . . . all Europe, except a part of
Muscovy. To this may be added a small part of Africa . . . and also a
good part of Asia. . . . For although the Egyptians, for instance, and the
[East] Indians are very black, or rather copper-coloured, that colour is
only an accident in them, and comes because they are constantly ex-
posed to the sun; and for those individuals who take care of themselves,
and who are not obliged to expose themselves so often as the lower
class, are not darker than many Spaniards. It is true that most Indians
have something very different from us in the shape of their face, and in
their colour which often comes very near to yellow; but that does not

seem enough to make them a species apart, or else it would be necessary to make one of the Spaniards, another of the Germans, and so on with several other nations of Europe.

Under the second species I put the whole of Africa, except the coasts I have spoken of. What induces me to make a different species of the Africans, are 1. Their thick lips and squab noses, there being very few among them who have aquiline noses or lips of moderate thickness. 2. The blackness which is peculiar to them, and which is not caused by the sun, as many think; for if a black African pair be transported to a cold country, their children are just as black, and so are all their descendants until they come to marry with white women. The cause must be sought for in the peculiar texture of their bodies, or in the seed, or in the blood — which last are, however, of the same colour as everywhere else. 3. Their skin, which is oily, smooth, and polished, excepting the places which are burnt with the sun. 4. The three or four hairs of beard. 5. Their hair, which is not properly hair, but rather a species of wool, which comes near to the hairs of some of our dogs; and, finally, their teeth whiter than the finest ivory, their tongue and all the interior of their mouth and their lips as red as coral.

The third species comprehends [the rest of Asia].... The people of all those countries are truly white; but they have broad shoulders, a flat face, a small squab nose, little pig's-eyes long and deep set, and three hairs of beard.

The Lapps make the fourth species. They are little stunted creatures with thick legs, large shoulders; short neck, and a face elongated immensely; very ugly and partaking much of the bear....

As to the Americans, they are in truth most of them olive-coloured, and have their faces modelled in a different way from ours. Still I do not find the difference sufficiently great to make of them a peculiar species different from ours. Besides as in our Europe, the stature, turn of the face, the colour and the hair are generally very different, as we have said, so it is the same in other parts of the world; as for example, the blacks of the Cape of Good Hope seem to be of a different species to those from the rest of Africa. They are small, thin, dry, ugly, quick in running.

Richard Bradley (1666-1732) classified American Indians and Europeans as white, and distinguished between them by the presence or absence of beards:

I proceed to take notice of the several Kinds of Men, whose Difference is remarkable. We find five Sorts of Men; the White Men, which are Europeans, that have Beards; and a sort of White Men in America (as I am told) that only differ from us in having no Beards. The third sort are the Malatoes, which have their Skins almost of a Copper Colour, small Eyes, and strait black Hair. The fourth Kind are the Blacks, which have straight black Hair; and the fifth are the Blacks of Guiney, whose Hair is curl'd, like the Wool of a Sheep, which difference is enough to shew us their Distinctions; for, as to their Knowledge, I suppose there would not be any great Difference, if it was possible they could be all born of the same Parents, and have the same Education, they would vary no more in Understanding than Children of the same House.

The attempt to classify human beings, a preoccupation of the West since the late Renaissance, was systematized in the 18th century by Carl von Linne, commonly known as Linnaeus (1707-1778). Although in his original classification of man he paid little attention to sub-specific variation, except in a note referring to wild men and men with tails, in the 10th edition of *Systema Naturae* Linnaeus gave a more detailed description of human groups. Under *Homo sapiens* he includes various classifications of mythical monsters, but under the sub-specific classification *H. Diurnus* he includes the following categories: 1. *Ferus Americanus* ("reddish, choleric, erect. Hair black, straight, thick; Nostrils wide; Face harsh, Beard scanty. Obstinate, merry, free. Paints himself with fine red lines. Regulated by customs.") 2. *Europaeus* ("white, sanguine, muscular. Hair flowing, long. Eyes blue. Gentle, acute, inventive. Covered with close vestments. Governed by laws.") 3. *Asiaticus* ("sallow, melancholy, stiff. Hair black. Eyes dark. Severe, haughty, avaricious. Covered with loose garments. Ruled by opinions.") 4. *Afer* ("black, phlegmatic, relaxed. Hair black, frizzled. Skin silky. Nose flat. Lips tumid. Women without shame. Mammae lactate profusely. Crafty, indolent, negligent. Annoints himself with grease. Governed by caprice.")

Count de Buffon (1707-1788) introduced the term race in 1749 to distinguish 6 varieties of the human species on the basis of color, shape of the body, and disposition; variation, he said, was due to climate, food and manners.

> The climate may be regarded as the chief cause of the different colours of men. But food, though it has less influence upon colour, greatly affects the form of our bodies. Coarse, unwholesome, and ill prepared food, makes the human species degenerate. All those people who live miserably, are ugly and ill-made. . . . The air and the soil have great influence upon the figure of men, beasts, and plants. In the same province, the inhabitants of the elevated and hilly parts are more active, nimble, handsome, ingenious, and beautiful, than those who live in the plains, where the air is thick and less pure.

> The earth is divided into two great continents. The antiquity of this division exceeds that of all human monuments; and yet man is more ancient, for he is the same in both worlds. The Asiatic, the European, and the Negro, produce equally with the American. Nothing can be a stronger proof that they belong to the same family, than the facility with which they unite to the common stock. The blood is different, but the germ is the same. The skin, the hair, the features, and the stature, have varied, without any change in internal structure.

In 1775, the German philosopher Immanuel Kant (1724-1804) used the concept of race to describe four races of mankind, White, Negro, Hunnish and Hindu. In the same year, the German anatomist Johann Blumenbach (1752-1840) identified five races based on color: white, yellow, black, red and brown. He theorized that the white race was the primeval race.

Poliakov (1971) points out that by the 16th century, the West began to invent blackness as an attribute of slavery. Slavery was not a new phenomenon. What was new was to identify physical features to justify slavery. Native Americans were distinguished from sub-Saharan Africans, the former being identified as white. According to Poliakov (1971:135),

> ...a form of discrimination became apparent which was already perceptible in the first book about the New World (*De Orbe Novo* by Pietro d'Anghiera 1516) where "white" Indians were contrasted with "black" Ethiopians. It can also be seen in the first attempt at "racial classification" (by Francois Bernier in 1684) when the Indians were assimulated into the white race. This discrimination still finds an echo in every European language since the contacts between Europe and other continents gave rise, in the case of Indians, to terms like *metis* and *mestizo,* which is not in itself perjorative, while *mulatto* is derived from mule....

The use of color or racial differences to justify slavery did not exist before the West occupied the New World. As Stepan (1982:xi) points out:

> The absence of a slave system based on race [in ancient Greece and Rome and during the Middle Ages in Europe] was probably closely connected with another important facet of ancient slavery and ancient thought, namely the absence of any obvious colour or racial prejudice. Greeks and Romans were both curious and knowledgeable about peoples other than themselves living in the Mediterranean, in Asia Minor and in Africa. We know from artistic depictions from Greece and Rome, and from literary sources, that black Africans, usually referred to by the generic term "Ethiopians," were well known in ancient times. But a careful study of the sources has failed to reveal any marked racial or colour prejudice.

What is the validity of color as a criterion of classification? Students of human biology agree that color is a complex and misleading trait to use in the classification of human groups. The number of genes involved, their interaction with each other and the environment, makes the genetics of color a complex topic. Even the adaptive significance of color is not certain, although numerous plausible hypotheses have been proposed. Human geneticists of recent times usually avoid using color, head shape and other polygenic, plastic traits as classificatory devices, preferring traits such as blood type because they are not influenced by the environment, and because they constitute a knowable genetic system.

The fact of human variability, however it is measured, has little to do with the practice of using physical markers to distinguish types of people which are then ranked hierarchically. Physical variation always exists in wide-ranging, homoiothermic populations. Allelic variation is a biological fact; races, however, are cultural creations.

The Origin of the Concept of Race

In some of the quotes listed in the previous section, classifications of people were based on physical as well as cultural characteristics. It is not clear when the term "race" was first used to denote inheritance, as in offspring or people of the same stock. Scholars disagree as to the origin of the word. It did not exist in classical Latin or Greek but appears in the 16th century in Old Italian as *razza,* a term related to Middle French *race,* translated as "generation," and to Spanish and Portuguese *raza.* Some have traced it to the Arabic *ras,* others to the Latin word *ratio,* meaning "order," and to the Latin word *radix,* meaning "root." It appears in English in 1580 to refer to a breed or stock of animals; and in a book called *History of the Gwydir Family,* published in 1600, there is a reference to a "Prince of Wales of the Brittish race." (See Montagu 1965).

The implication that there might be groups of people who belong to different lines of descent would seem to conflict with the principle of monogenesis. Monogenesis, or single origin, implied unity of mankind. Within the interpretive framework of medieval Catholicism, all men were perceived to be products of a single act of creation that began with Adam and Eve; we are all God's children.

The controversy of monogenesis vs. polygenesis constituted both a theological and an anthropological problem. From the orthodox theological point of view, man was created in the image of God only once; human variations were caused by degeneration and the influence of the environment. Those who rejected monogenesis had to deal with the following questions: did God have more than one image? Were different types of men created in the different images of God? Such questions challenged theological assumptions about the nature of God and His perfection.

The human others, or the non-Western peoples from the theological perspective, were descendents of Cain or Ham or others who had defied God and had degenerated. Therefore, they were not participants in the unfolding of truth through history. In the universal history, the human other had no significance, except as a category of contrast, a category of timelessness, arrested in a state of no grace (White 1972; Friedman 1981).

Beginning in the 15th century when the Catholic church approved the enslavement of sub-Saharan Africans, the church essentially contributed to the origin of the modern idea of race. According to Ashley Montagu (1965:23),

In the year 1455 Pope Nicholas V, by decree, approved the subjugation of infidels to Christians. The immediate result of this decree was the conversion of a religious-social difference into a socioeconomic, but not yet a "racial," discrimination. The decree meant that official sanction had been given to the enslavement of Negroes, Indians, and other "infidels," so that salvation of their souls and their entrance into God's Kingdom could be assured. It is from this time, the year 1455, that the Portuguese trade in slaves, principally in Africa, began in earnest.

However, the atrocities committed by the Conquistadores in the New World resulted in a papal bull being issued by Pope Paul III in 1537 "condemning the enslavement of Indians, declaring it heresy to say that they were irrational and incapable of conversion. The Pope also tried to transfer spiritual authority over the Indians from the Spanish Inquisition, which was controlled by the Spanish crown, to the bishop, but without success." (Montagu 1965: 25)

A shift in conception of the non-Westerner accompanied the economic exploitation of colonialism. European domination of the New World had cognitive as well as economic and political consequences. For the first time the Europeans realized that these human others, previously described in amusing travelogues by voyagers to far-flung places, were going to be part of their universe, that the geographical boundaries of the European universe would henceforth incorporate these strange others. This was a new problem, requiring a shift in relationship and a new definition of the idea of monogenesis.

The treatment of the Indians caused numerous debates over its moral legitimacy. In 1550, Bartolome de las Casas (1476-1566) defended the Indians by debating the Aristotelian concept that some men were born to be slaves (which Aristotle apparently meant with reference to individuals rather than groups, but which came to be used by Europeans to justify colonialism). According to Lewis Hanke, in a book called *Aristotle and the American Indians* (1959:15),

> Mankind is one, and all men are alike in that which concerns their creation and all natural things, and no one is born enlightened. From this it follows that all of us must be guided and aided at first by those who were born before us. And the savage peoples of the earth may be compared to uncultivated soil that readily brings forth weeds and useless thorns, but has within itself such natural virtue that by labour and cultivation it may be made to yield sound and beneficial fruits.

The moral outrage of Las Casas and others like him had little effect on the developing concept of race, especially after slavery was firmly established in the Americas by the 18th century. In a new world where the Europeans, American Indians and Africans would all live together, the Europeans had to be invented as the truly human, as the owners and controllers of this new world, as those whose manifest destiny was to save, protect, and regulate, and also to destroy, the lives of the sub-human others. Despite the fact that sub-Saharan Africans were imported to Europe as slaves beginning in the middle of the 15th century, there was little difficulty in seeing them as humans. But by the end of the 15th century, when American Indians were brought to Europe, we find that a major cognitive shift had occurred. In the discussions of why American Indians did not look like Africans, we find a new type of explanation: they were all lumped together as peoples who looked different from Westerners; and all these non-Western others were lumped with monsters and cannibals, as abnormal others. The Africans and American Indians were not originally perceived as sub-human; the doctrine of monogenesis had included them in a definition of humanity. Gradually, however, they were invented as sub-humans.

To quote Hodgen (1964: 362-363):

> Seen through the deforming fantasies of Solinus, Mela, Isidore, Mandeville, and their ilk, they were introduced to the European public not as nature's noblemen, endowed with all the innate virtues, and living in romantic communion with rustic surroundings, but as half-human, hairy wild men, degraded by "dayly tumultes, fears, doubts, sispitions, and barbarous cruelties."

> ...In the *Esmeraldo de situ orbis,* written about 1505, Duarte Pacheco Pereira describes the Negroes on the west coast of Africa as dog-faced, dog-toothed people, satyrs, wild men, and cannibals....According to Captain John Lok who in 1554 was still surveying the cliches of Herodotean legend, the region known as Guinea was inhabited by Troglodites who fed upon serpents; by Blemmines who had eyes and mouths in their chests....By this process of condemnation, New World man or the naked and threatening savage took that place in thought which, during the Middle Ages, had been reserved for human monsters. If human, theirs was a degraded humanity.

By the late 17th century, belief in the existence of different races of men was firmly established. In some writings, such as those of Sir William Tyson and Sir William Petty, racial classifications went beyond mere description and began to take on the trappings of hierarchy as they were interpreted as missing links between animals and humans. But even without these examples the mere fact of the acceptance of such classifications provided a model for a stratified concept of races in the 18th century.

During the 18th-century Enlightenment, the equality of man and the importance of culture in shaping behavior were affirmed more than at any other time in Western history. It is difficult to realize that the great thinkers of this period whom we identify as the spokesmen for the unity of mankind, universal rationality, brotherhood and egalitarianism, were, at the same time, convinced of the existence of inferior races. The issue is not whether they were "racist" but whether, during the 18th century, the idea that humans could be separated into different physical-behavioral groups had taken firm hold on the imagination of the West. On the one hand, Enlightenment scholars insisted on the psychic unity of mankind and the role of culture in human behavior; on the other, they described differences in the dispositions and personalities of different races, and thought that Western man had distinctive national characteristics which were rooted in the biological history of the Western race.

The philosopher David Hume (1711-1776), in an article called "Of National Characters," says:

> I am apt to suspect the negroes and in general all the other species of men (for there are four or five different kinds) to be naturally inferior to the whites. There never was a civilized nation of any other complexion than white, or even any individual eminent either in action or speculation. No ingenious manufactures among them, no arts, no sciences. On the other hand, the most rude and barbarous of the whites, such as the ancient Germans, the present Tartars, have still something eminent about them, in their valour, form of government, or some other particular. Such a uniform and constant difference could not happen in so many countries and ages, if nature had not made an original distinction betwixt these breeds of men. Not to mention our colonies, there are Negroe slaves dispersed all over Europe, of which none ever discovered any symptoms of ingenuity, tho' low people, without education, will start up amongst us, and distinguish themselves in every profession. In Jamaica indeed they talk of one negroe as a man of parts and learning; but 'tis likely he is admired for very slender accomplishments like a parrot, who speaks a few words plainly.

The studies on "national character" which became popular in the United States during the 20th century stem from an orientation which emerged in the 18th century and is particularly noticeable in the writings of German scholars such as Johann Gottfried von Herder (1744-1803).

In sum, in the 17th and 18th centuries it became acceptable to talk about differences among human populations in biological terms rather than in religious or cultural terms. And as the institution of slavery became established in the United States and other New World nations, these racial classifications took on new significance.

The Invention of the Black Other

According to Nash (1974:162-163), the reaction of Europeans to Africans varied in relation to their prior experience in associating with dark-skinned peoples:

> Though all European countries regarded their civilization as vastly superior to African societies, the Spanish and Portuguese were long familiar with darker-skinned people through centuries of trade and war

> with people from the Mediterranean, Middle Eastern, and North Afri-
> can worlds. But the fair-skinned English, brought face to face with the
> literally black Africans, seem to have reacted in a particularly negative
> way.... In English usage black became a partisan word. A black sheep
> in the family, a black mark against one's name, a black day, a black
> look, a black lie, a blackguard, and a blackball all were expressions built
> into the cultural consciousness.... The symbology of color was equally a
> part of Iberian culture but its effects on racial consciousness were tem-
> pered by the long associations which the Spanish and Portuguese had
> had with darker-hued people.

Despite these variations in images of the black other, the fact remains
that discussions of human others were, by the 18th century, centered on the
relationship between blacks and whites. Was the sub-Saharan African the
"same" as the European white man? Some, such as Buffon, believed in
monogenesis and argued that Africans did not differ in morphology or
physiology from whites. Others, such as Edward Long, believed in polygenesis and argued that the African was a member of a separate species
(Long 1970:356). Some expressed ambivalence about the human status of
the African.

Why this preoccupation with the racially categorized black? The answer
lies not in the blackness of Africans but in the needs and actions of the
Europeans. The creation of the black other as a distinctive being, biologically and intellectually inferior to the Western white us, was linked with the
institution of slavery. Without slavery, the black other would have had no
more significance than any other racial type developed for purposes of
boundary-maintenance.

The controversy over monogenesis and polygenesis, which had been
raging since at least the 13th century when the authority of the Catholic
church began to decline, was now linked with the question of slavery. In
defense of the colonial practices of their respective countries, scholars used
the Aristotelian theory of natural slavery, or the theory that it was a
Christian's duty to bring salvation to the infidels. The theory of degeneracy
which had for centuries been the church's explanation for human failings
and differences was now applied to blacks, with all the negative connotations available in Western tradition. The black, in the context of slavery,
came to represent the epitome of racial differentness, the supreme contrast
by which Western man could compare and define himself.

The evidence which 18th-century scholars used to talk about the humanness of blacks was provided primarily by politicians, preachers and popular
writers in the United States who presented what they considered incontro-
vertible proof that the slave was incapable of education and other features
of civilization.

Not all Americans supported this version of the black other. Thomas
Jefferson, after becoming acquainted with the black mathematician and

inventor, Benjamin Banneker, concluded that there was no difference between the mental capacities of blacks and whites. In 1782 Jefferson wrote a ietter to Banneker to the effect that he had been wrong in attributing intellectual differences to the races, and that he believed in the common intellectual heritage of all races.

European scholars, however, had little opportunity to encounter a Banneker or experience directly the conditions of slavery, and some had monetary investments in slavery. The Africans posed a dilemma in the minds of the Enlightenment thinkers who had affirmed egalitarianism and knowledge through education. Uprooted from their cultural and institutional contexts and prevented from acquiring new structures in the New World, Africans were considered inferior because they had none. The conditions of slavery necessarily gave rise to an image of the African as irrational and incapable of education, as someone who did not share in psychic unity, who had never had a civilization of his own, and who was, ultimately, biologically different from Western man.

Some scholars, such as Hodgen (1964) and Stocking (1968), have argued that racism is essentially a 19th-century phenomenon. Stocking says that the racist theology of the inequality of the races was a Romantic and conservative reaction in the 19th century against the rationalist and liberal worldview of the 18th century. I would argue, however, that racial classifications and inequality were already present in the 17th and 18th centuries; the 19th century provided a biological model justifying the distinctions which had already been made. The development of the Darwinian model, advances in clinical medicine, statistics and other aspects of science, were all put to use in the study of human variation.

In the 19th century a number of books began to talk about the purity of races and the dangers in mixing them. Many stated explicitly that the white race was the only race that had achieved civilization, and that it was necessary to protect the white race and the white civilization from the non-white races. The myth of the Aryan race was developed and anti-Semitism was on the rise.

The myth of the Aryan race was propagated in particular by three writers: Count Joseph Arthur de Gobineau (1816-1882), Richard Wagner (1813-1883) and Houston Steward Chamberlain (1855-1927). Gobineau, a Frenchman, argued that the white race was superior and energetic, the yellow race stable and fertile, the black race artistic and sensual. The Aryans, who were the primordial whites, had mixed with the yellow race in Asia and Western Europe, and with the black race in southern Europe and the Mediterranean (Semitic speakers were, in his classification, a black race), and this mixing had caused the decline of civilization. Wagner, a German, wrote extensively on the ruin wrought by the Semitic race on the German Aryan race. Chamberlain, an Englishman who married Wagner's daughter, elaborated the theories of Gobineau and Wagner in a book on racial history published in 1899.

In all of these writings a link was forged between race, language and culture. Both language and culture were biologized, and racial-cultural histories became popular.

The black other, in this new era of scientific racism, was given special treatment. A few, such as James Cowles Pritchard (1786-1848) and Samuel Stanhope Smith (1750-1819), supported monogenesis and theorized that racial differences were superficial, caused primarily by environment. Smith (1810:191-194), for example, remarked that:

> I am inclined... to ascribe the apparent dullness of the negro principally to the wretched state of his existence first in his original country, where he is at once a poor and abject savage, and subjected to an atrocious despotism; and afterwards in those regions to which he is transported to finish his days in slavery, and toil. Genius, in order to its cultivation, and the advantageous display of its power, requires freedom; it requires reward, the reward at least of praise, to call it forth; competition to awaken its ardor; and examples both to direct its operations, and to prompt its emulation.

Pritchard theorized that early man was black, and that lighter pigmentation was a later development in the evolution of man.

However, most scholars in the 19th century provided "evidence" (often fabricated) from many sources to link race, language and culture in their construction of the black other (see Gould 1981 for a detailed discussion). Political theorists argued that the African lacked the rationality to acquire civilization. The "father of American physical anthropology," Samuel George Morton, did skull measurements to prove that Negroes were inferior to Caucasians. The 19th century was full of measurements of facial angles which placed the Africans at the polar extreme of the Europeans (Stanton 1960; Haller, Jr. 1970). In the same tradition, an article in the *American Anthropologist* by Edward Spitzka (1903) suggested that the brain weight of a Zulu is midway between that of a gorilla and the European scientist Cuvier. Clinical medicine was also put to the task of creating the black other, as Stewart C. Gilman suggests (1982:38):

> The racism of the late nineteenth and twentieth century is not simply a bastardization of evolutionary theory. Many of its assumptions are based on phrenological studies conducted during the period of the American Civil War and continuing through the early part of the twentieth century. Most of the racial implication of these studies resulted from an amalgamation of degeneration theory and phrenology, with a liberal dose of social Darwinism and a dash of evolutionary theory. This recipe was concocted for the most part in Southern Medical Journals. These journals were so preoccupied with race and racial inferiority, that an impartial observer might conclude that the only prevalent disease in the Southern part of the United States was race.

Blackness was not only moral and intellectual inferiority but disease. Medical evidence was used to argue that blackness could sometimes be cured; that the black race was an inferior breed that was dying out; that the deterioration of offspring in the black race was manifested in higher rates of insanity, immorality and criminality (Brandt 1978).

Such views continue in the 20th century. Injection of blacks with syphilis was condoned because they were considered so immoral that they would be certain to catch it anyway (cf. Jones 1981). Arthur Jensen of the University of California at Berkeley is the major proponent today of the belief that Africans (except for those with many "white" genes) lack the capacity for Western civilization which requires rational, analytic thought. In support of this thesis, which echoes the West's view of the black other since the development of slavery, he marshalls the statistics of IQ measurement. (See Gould 1981).

It is beyond the scope of this book to debate the issue of race and intelligence; a host of social and psychological scientists have challenged Jensen and his supporters. The issue here is the Western creation of the black other.

The West continues to use the concept of race, despite the fact that it has been repeatedly demonstrated that the concept does not approximate or identify the reality of human variation. The typological thinking and the use of the concept of race imply that there were at one time pure races. Without such an assumption it would be illogical to have racial classifications. Thus the modern use of the concept of race and racial classifications are in no way different from the writings of Gobineau, Wagner and Chamberlain. The standard typology identifies three or four major groupings, despite the fact that intra-group variation often exceeds inter-group variation.

The typological thinking of the racial classifications acquired a boost in the 20th century through the writings of Harvard physical anthropologists such as Ernest Hooton and Carleton S. Coon who in the 1960's proposed that polygenesis was in fact valid, and that different races evolved into full humanness at different times. As might be anticipated, he identified the black race as having acquired sapienness last.

An alternative model to the typological studies of human variation is often called the clinal approach. The clinal approach is predicated on the principle that there is a graded variation in the distribution of traits. In order to study variation, one must chart the occurrence of certain traits in higher percentages in certain regions, and try to suggest the reasons for their variation in allelic frequency. Traits are studied separately, not packaged in some archetypal "pure race," the boundaries of which would, at any rate, be impossible to decipher.

The clinal approach is accepted by most physical anthropologists as valid, but the concept of race is also used. The reason it continues to be used is that the West needs the concept of race; it continues to pay for the research which supports separation of the West from the black other.

I suggest that but for the existence of the symbol of the black other, the concept of race would not have acquired the importance it did in the 19th and 20th centuries. I also suggest that but for the existence of that symbol, scholars would have stopped using the concept of race long ago. It has become the central image of the non-Western other by which the West distinguishes itself.

Chapter Nine

The Mythology of the Ethnographic Other in the Western Tradition

The Invention of the Ethnographic Other

Ethnography in its ideal form involves the description of everyday life of a human group in its totality, through observation and through approximation of the cultural categories that are used by the group to organize the different domains of existence and experience. Ethnography, however, must have relevance for the audience of the ethnographer; perhaps it gives the reader a feeling for the people, like a good novel; or the information is useful for administrators or those who govern; or it addresses certain controversies about the validity of certain practices in the ethnographer's society.

Anthropologists accept ethnographies as a valid mode of knowing cultural reality. They use them in comparative studies and in discussing or explaining the nature of human institutions and human nature. In the process of being used this way, ethnographies are transformed into reified entities; they become timeless and the people become ethnographic others. This anthropological invention is necessary for the ethnographer to answer questions about the past, present and future of his own society. In other words, an ethnography is an invention, a description of a society that has remained unchanged and will remain unchanged; in such form, it lends itself to theoretical treatment, as per whatever anthropological theory is current or debated. This can occur because the ethnographic other is not only spatially distant but also temporally distant and has meaning in relation to the ethnographer's society by fusing the temporal and spatial distances to meet the concerns and needs of the ethnographer's society.

Johannes Fabian, in his book entitled *Time and the Other: How Anthropology Makes its Object* (1983: 147-148) observes:

> ...nineteenth-century anthropology sanctioned an ideological process
> by which relations between the West and its Other, between anthro-

pology and its Object, were conceived not only as difference, but as distance in space *and* Time.

When, in the course of disciplinary growth and differentiation, evolutionism was attacked and all but discarded as the reigning paradigm of anthropology, the conceptions it had helped to establish remained unchanged.

As soon as it is realized that fieldwork is a form of communicative interaction with an Other, one that must be carried out coevally, on the basis of shared intersubjective Time and intersocietal contemporaneity, a contradiction had to appear between research and writing because anthropological writing had become suffused with strategies and devices of an allochronic discourse.

Long (1978:406) notes that anthropological "data on the *other* that was to be interpreted came from those removed in time and/or in space. The problem of knowledge thus constitute a structure of distance and relationships. Objectivity as a scientific procedure allied itself with the neutrality of the distancing in time and space."

Thus the anthropologist, in his creative interpretation and use of the ethnographic other, is more like the artist who constructs a collage from items collected from different times and places to meet the critical needs of his day than he is like the scientist who begins with an external scene and tries to define the objective functional connections between its parts. The anthropologist in fact does both, but gains his legitimacy more from the former than from the latter.

Renaissance Beginnings of the Ethnographic Tradition

The West is not unique in describing the customs of alien peoples. All imperialist and colonial governments probably encouraged the collection of information about the people they conquered or colonized. The Greeks had a tradition of describing the aliens, and so did the Romans. The Chinese had a tradition of describing those they had colonized or those with whom they had political and economic relationships (Needham 1959: 508-514). Arab nations also had a tradition of description. For two hundred years the British described and analyzed the customs of those they had conquered and colonized, not for anthropological insights but for controlling the colonies, an activity which later acquired anthropological significance. But these descriptions should not be taken to mean that the foundations of anthropology were in imperialism and colonialism.

As I have argued previously, the West's preoccupation with the abnormal during the Middle Ages provided a contrast for opposing the true self and the untrue self; I have suggested that this dichotomy reflected the restrictive mythology of the Judeo-Christian orientation. During the Renaissance, descriptions of non-Western peoples took on significance as mythological representations to understand the nature of the West and humankind. Gruber (1973:32), comparing earlier writings of non-Western peoples with European descriptions during the Renaissance, comments,

> As interesting as these early accounts are and as important as they can be for the historical reconstruction and validation of ethnological conclusions, they lack any sense of anthropological problem. As in other areas of science, that sense of problem in anthropology seems to be a unique product of the later European cultural tradition.

What is this "sense of anthropological problem"? What was it that sparked "the Renaissance passion for collecting," as Gruber says (1973:39), which promoted "a genre, the literary collection of customs" that was "analogous to the cabinets of artifacts and specimens or the zoological and botanical gardens for an assemblage and display of biological exotica"? As Gruber further says (1973:39),

> Although the next two centuries were to see the continuance of the medieval pattern of describing the unnatural as natural, and the monsters as real, *by the end of the sixteenth century, there was already firmly established an ethnographic tradition for the collection of customs of the diverse peoples.... [emphasis mine]*

Participant Observation and Objectivity

Until the late 19th century, most anthropological data were collected by missionaries, travellers, and amateur collectors, but in the late 19th and early 20th centuries, field expeditions were organized specifically to collect anthropological data: in 1873 the German ethnologist Adolf Bastian organized the Loango expedition to West Africa; Franz Boas took part in the Jesup North Pacific Expedition in 1897; the Englishman A.C. Haddon led the Torres Straits Expedition organized in 1898; and in 1904 Leo Frobenius, the German ethnologist, organized the Inner-African expedition. In the Americas, systematic descriptions began in the 18th century, although a few ethnographies had been done during the preceding two centuries. Jesuit priests, government officials and others made detailed and sensitive recordings of American Indian cultural traditions. Collection of data in India was done primarily for government use during the 19th century.

Participant observation, the practice of an individual living for long periods of time in close association with a particular group, learning and describing its language and customs, became common in the 20th century; and ever since Malinowski extolled the virtues of the method, this method of acquiring data from an alien culture has been regarded as uniquely anthropological, a hallowed trademark of anthropological fieldwork.

Participant observation, however, is a recent phenomenon, an offshoot of the Romantic movement of the early 20th century in which the phenomenological approach validated personal experience as a mode of knowledge. As many recent books have indicated, field experience introduces the student to the reality of cultural relativism, and makes the student self-reflective and furthers his understanding of his own culture. "Culture shock" as experienced by the novice anthropologist has an inherent romantic appeal to Western audiences.

Although participant observation in the field is often referred to as a "rite of passage," few have examined the sociological dimensions of this ritual phenomenon in detail. The use of the term itself is somewhat confusing. It has been used to imply that field experience is essential for entry into the ranks of anthropology, and in this sense the emphasis is placed on physical hardships and other trying experiences encountered in the field; such experiences facilitate the emergence of a common bond among anthropologists. But the term is usually used to mean that a student's first field experience has an impact profound enough to create an *existential transformation*. Here the emphasis is placed on what occurs to the *self* in the field rather than whether or not field experience leads to the student's acceptance as an anthropologist. What appears to be relevant is the experiential, psychological facet of participant observation. Sociological factors usually discussed in the studies of rituals of passage have not been applied to the analysis of participant observation as a rite of passage.

An important sociological feature of participant observation in 20th century anthropology has to do with the long period of formal education typical of Western and Western-influenced societies, which itself may be regarded as a rite of passage. The secularization of education during the Renaissance in the West (in the wake of commercialism which necessitated secular education) generated a change in prior concepts of education, shifting educational institutions from bastions of conservatism to agents of innovation. Students of the 20th century are in the forefront of change in the society. They have access to power through the acquisition of knowledge, but this power is not exploited until the student ceases to be a student. Their studentship is a rite of passage between childhood and adult status; and while they are still students, their role is ambiguous. (Some who continue to be "students," or intellectuals, continue to have ambiguous status in society.) The ambiguity of their position, their lack of an adult social position, makes it possible for them to be less rigid in matters of hierarchy, etc. A society must be wealthy to afford to support for a long time a large number of persons who have ambiguous status.

Although most anthropologists say that they had excellent rapport with their subjects and were "accepted" as members of the society they studied, their position in that society is ambiguous. The common quip that a female anthropologist is a male in the field illustrates sexual ambiguity. Although they may have been "adopted" (in the sense that they acquired a ritual mother, son, sister, brother or father), the fact that they were allowed to participate in almost all societal activities implies that their participation was not restricted to that of an actual societal member locked into dyadic role relationships with a mother, son, sister, brother or father. In order to gather data effectively in the field, the anthropologist's position (like that of a ritual neophyte, as Turner 1969 describes it) is "necessarily ambiguous." The anthropologist slips "through the network of classifications that normally locate states and positions in cultural space" and in relation to the group studied the anthropologist is in a state of liminality with a mind that is "a blank slate, on which is inscribed the knowledge and wisdom of the group."

The analogy between the anthropologist and the neophyte in puberty rituals breaks down in one important respect: whereas the neophyte acquires the wisdom of the group in order to occupy a particular position in the society, the anthropologist acquires the wisdom but retains the ambiguous state of existence. The anthropologist does not become a native but is forever in the process of becoming a native. He is there not to become a member of that society, but to satisfy the needs dictated by his own traditions.

Why, in turn, is the anthropologist tolerated by the group he studies? How is a person whose position is ambiguous allowed to live with a group which structures relationships and is afraid of ambiguity? I suggest that groups perceive in the anthropologist a source of power that is external to the group, and through their consent to be studied they seek to participate in and acquire the power of the anthropologist.

There are numerous ways by which this perception of the anthropologist is perpetuated. Anthropologists manifest their relative affluence by supplying food and drinks, medicine, transport, etc.; they also serve as symbols of the dominant Western society. Anthropological gadgets such as the camera, tape recorder and radio are by themselves signs of power. In peasant cultures, some secure money from the anthropologist through begging or employment, and some aspire to go with the anthropologists when they return to the West.

Anthropologists may occupy a relatively low status in the West but to members of the society they study they are direct representatives of the dominant society. The cultures studied by anthropologists are those that for the most part have been subjected to Western influence either through colonialism or economic imperialism.

Apart from the material affluence which is a major source of power, another feature of power is related to those aspects of physical appearance and demeanor on which members of a society may place high or low value. One aspect of stratification within a society, and dominant-subordinate relationships between societies, is that persons and groups with high status provide a model for ideal standards of beauty and proper behavior. The West, having become the dominant culture, is not only looked upon as the most powerful economically and militarily, but also as the standard for ideal forms of physical beauty and proper behavior. White skin color, Western mannerisms and Western language are passports for anthropologists to function in non-Western societies in spite of their ambiguous state.

How do non-Western anthropologists acquire the power to study their own societies? The same principle of dominance operates, for it is the more Westernized members of those societies, the urban, educated, Hindu, Chinese and Japanese anthropologists, who study the socially inferior tribal populations and peasants of their respective countries.

It is reasonable to suggest that the ritual of participant observation can occur only in the context of a dominant and subordinate relationship between societies, and that only members of the dominant society can perform the ritual. This would indicate that an anthropological study is impossible unless members of the studied society emulate and seek to acquire the power of the anthropologist. Participant observation in an affluent, Western community (or any society which possesses already the symbols of power with which anthropologists are identified) would be enormously difficult.

The ambiguity of anthropologists in the field introduces a psychological bias to their study. Because of the fact that anthropologists do not become natives but are always in the process of becoming natives, they establish no meaningful relationships, i.e., in the manner in which certain relationships are meaningful to the natives (with sentiments and responsibilities). In order to gather data concerning meaningful relationships, anthropologists, who start with the premise that human acts are cultural expressions, must ask informants "what the acts mean to them," or "why a particular activity is conducted in a particular manner," and observe recurring or repetitive behavior. It is up to the anthropologist to interpret whether the statements of the natives and their behavior mean the same thing. His abstractions are *conceptual* schema which are intelligible and relevant to the academic community. *In other words, the social and cultural reality constructed by the anthropologist is actually a portrait of his own psychological reality, as dictated by the ideas that are considered meaningful to him and his audience.*

Data on the Ethnographic Other as Capital

Anthropological data, i.e., the data on non-Western peoples, can be viewed as capital investment in two ways. The data constitute an investment for the collector: the collector's career and material prosperity depend on how effective he or she is in selling them. The data also constitute an investment for the society which supports the collector, particularly the government, agency or university which funds or condones the collection of data: the data provide information that can be used for achieving positive or negative results in the relationship between the government of the anthropologist and the government of the data-society. The histories of particular leading departments of anthropology are to some extent a history of their special relationships with particular data-societies. The United States government has invested heavily in anthropological research on American Indians, who have constituted the prime source of anthropological data for the past 200 years. In recent times, South India has become the data-society for many American anthropologists. The British were explicit in emphasizing the significance of anthropological data in improving the effectiveness of their colonial government. The British engaged in the most exhaustive collection of anthropological data, particularly from India, for over 100 years during the 19th and early 20th centuries. Dozens of manuals and ethnographic volumes describing caste and tribal customs were published at public expense. The expenses were justified as contributing to the maintenance of order. To a lesser extent the same colonial governmental policy was adopted in Africa. Different nation-states of the West have "cornered" or "territorialized" different peoples of the non-West as their data, their use of these peoples reflecting their social traditions, philosophies and political purposes.

On the whole, there has been a progressive "anthropologization" of the non-West since the late Renaissance. That is, the West has proceeded to render the non-West the object of study in ways that suit the needs of the West; the non-West has been invented or created to answer questions of importance in health, economics, politics or religion in the Western tradition. The subordinated or colonized peoples of the non-West seldom have the political/military power to prevent being anthropologized. As Everett C. Hughes points out in his paper, "Who Studies Whom?" (1974:30),

> The person doing the studying used to simply arrogate to himself and his kind the license to study the Other. The studied were helpless to prevent being studied except by the means common to all humans of shutting their mouths, by not communicating, by misinforming in one way or other.

In the anthropologizing of the non-West, anthropologists seek to solve the problems of the Western tradition, gathering data that would help the West to answer certain questions. Although cross-cultural research is usually presented as an exercise in science which speaks to the general concerns of humanity (as expressed by statements such as "science is in the service of humanity" and "science serves mankind"), it is standard procedure in applying for grants to fund cross-cultural research to explain how the research will shed light on a particular phenomenon relevant to the funding society. The foci of anthropological research shift in response to the changing needs of Western society.

For about two hundred years, when Western scholars were reacting against religion as an irrational survival of early human development, a primary concern of anthropology was the scientific study of religion. When moral and social philosophers were concerned with defining human nature, anthropology focused on discovering the true nature of non-Western human groups. During the past two decades, as drugs became a major concern in Western society, anthropology provided cross-cultural descriptions of transcendental experiences. Today the West's preoccupation with sexual roles, nutrition and physical fitness is reflected in anthropological interest in medical anthropology.

When members of subordinate societies pursue the study of anthropology, they borrow the concepts and methods developed in the Western dominant society. Thus the phenomena they seek to explain and the problems that engage their attention are not relevant to their societies but to Western society. For example, as a result of the West's interest in the drug phenomenon, non-Western anthropologists have become interested in the use of drugs, although drugs have been used in these societies for hundreds of years. Members of subordinate societies are dependent on the decisions made by members of Western society as to what is relevant, relevance being determined by what occurs in Western society.

Francis L.K. Hsu (1973) recently voiced the opinion that a deep-seated prejudice exists in anthropology against non-Western views and interpretations of man, and that this prejudice "has in some areas warped the intellectual progress" of American anthropology. But according to my argument, the very nature of anthropology derives from interpreting non-Western cultures in the Western cultural context. Eliminating "prejudice" would be eliminating anthropology.

Interpretive Data and Allegorical Data

The following sub-sections provide examples or "case studies" to illustrate the mythological functions of the ethnographic other in the West.

a. The Cannibal Other

William Arens, in an important book, *The Man-Eating Myth: Anthropology and Anthropophagy* (1979), has pointed out that all the documented evidence of cannibalism except for one instance, in which it is probable that the anthropologist mistook wood ash for the ash of a human corpse, was hearsay evidence, thus raising the possibility that the cannibal other is a Western creation. The functions of such an image of the ethnographic other are suggested in a passage by Herder (1885:329):

> Is there any species of barbarity, to which some man, some nation, nay frequently a number of nations, have not accustomed themselves; so that

many, perhaps most, have even fed on the flesh of their fellow-crea-
tures? Is there a wild conception the mind can frame which has not been
actually rendered sacred by hereditary tradition, in one place or another?...I am persuaded, no form of human manners is possible, which
some nation, or some individual, has not adopted.

In other words, cannibalism represents the ultimate statement of the
extremes of human possibility which the ethnographic other offers to the
West. The icons and descriptions of American Indians and Africans as
cannibals were popular in the West from the 16th century. See Bucher
(1981) for an illuminating interpretation of the iconography of human
others in the Western tradition.

b. The Dreaming Other

In June of 1978, the magazine *Human Nature* reported that a group of
film makers, inspired by the anthropological writings of Kilton Stewart,
had gone to Malaysia to record dream discussions among the Temiar. The
Temiar, according to Stewart, were reputed to discuss dreams actively and
make use of them in culturally constructive ways. Patricia Garfield's book,
Creative Dreaming, was stimulated by Stewart's description. To the film
makers' amazement, no extensive interest in dreams was found among the
Temiars.

> Bloch and Boatwright's visit to the Temiar occurred 40 years after
> Stewart spent time with the tribe, and there have been vast changes in
> Temiar life in the interim, but not enough to wipe out what seemed to be
> a major part of their culture. In addition, the film makers were eager to
> confirm Stewart's findings. As Bloch says, "Given that our visit to the
> jungle was relatively brief, that our movements were restricted, and that
> Stewart was there some forty years before us, there still seems to be a
> huge gap."

It is rare in anthropological research that more than one anthropologist
studies the same group, and anthropologists often identify a particular
group as "their" people and jealously guard their right to be the phenomenological interpreter of the reality which they represent. If a group does
happen to be studied by someone else and the interpretation is different, the
possibility is usually raised that the society has changed. Anthropologists
still debate whether the enormous difference in the interpretations of Oscar
Lewis and Robert Redfield concerning Tepotzlan is due to culture change or
to differences in their theoretical orientations. The most recent debate on
this problem concerns the work of Margaret Mead in Samoa. Derek
Freeman (1983) who studied Samoa for a long time suggests that her report-
ing was both inaccurate and theoretically biased.

One can see the same conflict in the account of the Temiar. The West has
an investment in the ethnographic other as a being who, unlike Western
man, remains in close touch with his dreams, intuitions, and other

expressions of irrationality excluded from the West's conception of the true self.

c. The Magical Other

Arguments about the "field data" provided by Carlos Castaneda may be examined in the same light. Whether Castaneda really knew a Yaqui sorceror named Don Juan, or whether he "invented" his ethnographic data as some have suggested (de Mille 1980), the popularity of his books reflects the fact that they satisfied a Western need. They support the image of the human other as having an intimacy with magic and monsters which the West is not seen to have. Castaneda's defenders do not speak to the factual nature of his writings but to their importance as "allegories" for understanding religion and human nature. The primary function of anthropology as a humanistic discipline which provides meaning rather than a "science" which records factual data is in this case overwhelmingly clear.

d. The Rape-Free Other

The rise of feminist concerns in the West has been accompanied by anthropological studies which seek to probe the range of human possibilities offered by the ethnographic other with special attention paid to the way different societies handle male-female relationships.

A series of exchanges in *Science 82* illustrates the interest in studies on rape in other cultures. In October of 1982, Peggy Sanday described her findings that rape was a product of male-dominated, aggressive cultures. Subsequent letters published in the magazine argued the issue back and forth. Several decades ago, the American preoccupation with male-female relationships and definitions was phrased differently by Margaret Mead, who was answering the need of Americans concerned with the biological or cultural basis of sex roles.

e. The Whole Other

Many more examples may be provided to illustrate that anthropological inquiry is not so much an objective, naturalistic science of man as it is a Western quest for meaning of contrast and integration. Margaret Mead, one of the foremost anthropologists of this century, popularized anthropology in books which stated explicitly that the non-West could be used as an experimental laboratory in which the West could learn of the malleability of human nature. In *Coming of Age in Samoa* (1949), she was concerned with whether the restlessness of American adolescents was a function of biological maturation or cultural conditioning.

In *Sex and Temperament in Three Primitive Societies* (1963:xiv), she says,

> I set as my problem a study of the conditioning of the social personalities of the two sexes, in the hope that such an investigation would throw some light upon sex-differences. I shared the general belief of our soci-

ety that there was a natural sex-temperament which could at the most only be distorted or diverted from normal expression. I was innocent of any suspicion that the temperaments which we regard as native to one sex might instead be mere variations of human temperament, to which the members of either or both sexes may, with more or less success in the case of different individuals, be educated to approximate.

In a more general sense, ethnographic data represent not only a reservoir of human possibility into which the West may dip in search of various types of information; they also are given concrete image in the symbol of the whole other. Unlike the fragmented, distintegrating, anomic structure of Western society, the non-West represents an integrated Gemeinschaft, the ultimate community to which the alienated Westerner (in particular the anthropologist, who is often conceived of as promoting, through his discipline, "institutionalized alienation") may go.

Part III
Inventing Anthropology

I have suggested in this book that modern anthropology is, at the epistemological level, rooted in the Judeo-Christian orientation, and is part of the Western cultural tradition. Stated differently, anthropology is a cultural invention of human nature, necessitated because of certain distinctive features of selfhood in the Western tradition. The notion of viewing anthropology as a social or cultural phenomenon of the Western tradition is not new. For example, Dolgin, Kemnitzer, and Schneider (1977:6-7) in their book of readings on *Symbolic Anthropology* suggest that "...no culture other than our own—for, indeed, anthropology is an inextricable artifact of Western European culture—has produced an inquiry of the scale or the nature of anthropology."

The development and the maintenance of anthropology cannot be fully grasped without a study of the non-rational, the symbols and myths, and of the selfhood within the Western tradition. In short we must understand what the discourse on human others meant to the Western tradition. The theoretical shifts and the different preoccupations with different human others need to be examined in relation to the needs and concerns of the different generations of the Western tradition. What is relevant anthropological data for one generation may not be so for another generation.

This does not mean that we must neglect to study the power relationships between the West and the non-West; in fact, it is necessary to develop an orientation that might be called the "anthropology of history," a study which examines the historical patterns of relationships between the West and the non-West, and which also investigates how history is constructed in different societies to explain these relationships. I discuss this in Chapter Eleven.

Chapter Ten

The Anthropology of Anthropology

Anthropology in Culture

The anthropologists Irving Hallowell (1965:24-38) and Dell Hymes (1962) were among the first to suggest that anthropology could be conceptualized and studied as a cultural aspect of the Western tradition. Hallowell observed that the study of anthropology as a history of organized inquiries should be supplemented with a study of anthropology's "roots in a wider context," and that "an anthropological approach to the history of anthropology in Western culture suggests that this history should be set squarely within the cultural context of Western civilization." Hallowell advocated the investigation of the linkages between anthropology and other disciplines, and noted that the method of ethnoscience, i.e., the analysis of the organization of cultural categories, should be applied to understand differences and similarities in the anthropological paradigms of different cultural traditions and to understand the temporal differences in the anthropological paradigms of the Western tradition. He was of the view that a cognitive shift from the conception of humanity in terms of theological or culturally constituted folk models to the conception of humanity in terms of scientific models occurred in the Western tradition in relation to the historical contact of diverse peoples.

Regna Darnell (1974) recommends the methodology of the sociology of knowledge to understand the relationship between anthropology and the sociocultural context in which it arose. She correctly notes that "Like practitioners of any discipline, we [anthropologists] exist in a social milieu that cannot, by definition, be static.... From the historical point of view, anthropology is that which anthropologists do because they are members of an historically constituted cultural tradition that we call anthropology." (1974:2)

The theoretical approach of the sociology of knowledge helps us to understand the social roots or foundations of knowledge, the interdependence of social structures and belief systems of a society, as well as to promote relativism of knowledge systems which claim to be religious or scientific "truths." Historicist scholarship, which many historians such as George Stocking, Jr. (1968) have deployed to understand the internal logic of anthropology, helps us understand past periods without imposing the value judgments of the present.

In examining the theoretical shifts in anthropology during the past 200 years, we can fruitfully employ the perspectives of the sociology of knowledge and historicism. The various anthropological orientations such as the evolutionism of the 18th and 19th centuries, historical particularism, diffusionism, configurationism and social-structural functionalism of the 20th century can be seen as corresponding to the socio-political context in which they became popular. (See Chapter Two for a discussion of different national-anthropological orientations which emerged in the 20th century.)

The Cultural Constitution of Modern
Anthropology in the Western Tradition

In discussing the beginnings of anthropology as the "scientific" study of humankind, reference is usually made to the theory of Thales of Miletus that life originated in the seas, to Democritus and his atoms, to Lucretius and the first law of thermodynamics, and the like. It is often suggested that the developmental, change-oriented model of the Greek and Roman traditions was rejected during the Medieval Period of the Western tradition and then reasserted itself during the Renaissance, giving rise to anthropology, biology and other naturalistic, developmentally oriented disciplines, which thereby must trace their origins to Greek and Roman times. Such an origin of anthropology is viewed as the scientific heritage of the discipline.

Although a naturalistic view of the universe and of humankind is a necessary part of anthropology, such a view by itself is not sufficient to explain the emergence and maintenance of modern anthropology. Several ancient Western and non-Western traditions had a naturalistic view of the universe and some alternated (and still alternate today) between a naturalistic and theological view of the universe. But none of these traditions produced an orientation towards the study of humankind which is similar to that of modern anthropology. Anthropology was born as a disciplinary inquiry in the 16th and 17th centuries during the late Renaissance of the West, was cultivated during the 18th-century Western Enlightenment, took on aspects of Romanticism, and became professionalized in the 19th century. That it emerged then and was sustained thereafter cannot be explained by referring to its naturalistic orientation.

Most textbooks emphasize the naturalistic orientation of anthropology and the comparison of the customs of other peoples, linking this orientation with Greco-Roman times. Most, for example, refer to the Greek historian Herodotus of the 5th century B.C., who described the customs of non-Greeks, as an early anthropologist (Malefijt 1974: Voget 1975; Honigmann 1976). I disagree with this historical version of modern anthropology. The comparative method of anthropology which evolved during the Renaissance was different and distinctive from that of Herodotus. Even though Herodotus compared customs of non-Greek peoples to establish functional equivalents, his writings and the writings of others like him were used by the Greek intellectuals as a source of amusement rather than as an avenue of truth about what constituted humanness. (Aristotle, for example, defined anthropology as "gossip.") To the Greeks, Herodotus' writings about other peoples did not constitute an avenue of knowledge about the nature of humankind. The Greeks had their own anthropology, that is, their own definitions of humankind and what it meant to be human; their anthropology was developed through introspection and through empirical observation, and was not based on the knowledge of the human other. Romans also described the customs of non-Romans; Pliny, Mela, Solinus, Tacitus and others produced descriptions based on observation and hearsay. An intellectual tradition of writing natural histories and compendia of all known "facts" about the universe, like the contemporary "People's Almanac" or "Ripley's Believe-it-or not," has continued from the Greco-Roman times to the present in the West. In the Medieval Period, scholars such as Isidore, the Bishop of Seville (7th century) and Bartholomaeus Angelicus (13th century) produced several volumes; also, John Mandeville's and Marco Polo's travelogues (13th and 14th centuries), as well as missionary description of the customs, particularly the religious practices of the Mongols in the 13th century, were published. (See Hodgen 1964:17-107 for detailed discussion.)

Description of alien customs was not an exclusive activity of the Western tradition. Travellers, traders, missionaries and administrators of several different cultural traditions provided descriptions of alien peoples and cultures at different times in the past 2,000 years. For example, the Chinese and the Muslims produced lengthy reports on the customs of Asian Indians and Africans. In the 14th century, the historian/sociologist/administrator, Ibn Khaldun, described the Arabs; there were others like him before and after.

But description of alien customs or peoples by itself is not anthropological data. What distinguishes the information as anthropological is how the information is used, how functional it is in constructing images of humankind in the Western tradition. Of course, the data collected by missionaries, colonial administrators and others, for reasons such as to proselytize, to govern or to entertain, can be transformed into anthropological data.

Anthropological studies are not simply analytical orientations that can be identified as comparative or cross-cultural psychology, sociology, or political science. Psychologists, sociologists and political scientists may use anthropological data or may even engage in fieldwork among alien peoples to test various hypotheses or to construct various models of behavior and development. But they do not, from their disciplinary perspective, define the characteristics of other peoples and then relate these characteristics to the characteristics of us to produce various models of human integration. There are, in many instances, scholars who do not confine their theoretical perspectives to any particular disciplinary bounds and a sharp distinction cannot be made when cross-cultural or comparative studies are undertaken; the use of the Human Relations Area Files, the repository of data on peoples and customs, to discover causal relationships or correlations between institutions, beliefs, etc., has an interdisciplinary orientation. Also, it may be pointed out that, until the 19th century when the social and behavioral sciences became professionalized, scholars were, for the most part, involved in what we would call today multi-disciplinary studies. Most of the scholars from the late Renaissance were concerned with the human others, and the various compartmentalized disciplines of contemporary universities all claim, justifiably, the same scholars as the founding fathers of their respective disciplines. Those disciplines that deal with the study of social processes have, to some extent, continued to be linked.

In what period the "beginning" of anthropology is located depends on what the author considers typical or distinctive of the discipline. Voget (1975:3) cites four criteria which can be used to identify the presence of a discipline:

1. The exponents of a discipline usually express a strong sense of difference by contrasting their special subject matter with that of others.
2. A special theory of reality and of "causal" explanation is claimed, even though these may not be made fully explicit.
3. A claim is made to a distinctive methodology.
4. A special set of factual materials is assembled that contrasts with those usually employed in related disciplines.

I have argued that it is the use of the human other as a comparative focus in Western man's search for insights into the nature of humankind which makes anthropology a distinctive discipline. Applying my criterion of distinctiveness, I have located the beginning of anthropology in the late Renaissance. Before explaining my reasons for doing so, I will examine contrasting histories by both historians and anthropologists which trace anthropology's birth to the Greco-Roman period or to the Enlightenment period. I will comment on the studies of two particular scholars who are representative of these two different interpretive preferences.

Margaret Hodgen's *Early Anthropology in the Sixteenth and Seventeenth Centuries,* which was published in 1964, locates the beginning of anthropology in the Greco-Roman period. According to her, 19th-century professionalized anthropology was "old wine in a new bottle": all the ideas which had become anthropological concepts and theories in the 19th century had existed before; there was nothing new under the Greek sun.

In contrast, Marvin Harris' *Rise of Anthropological Theory,* which was published in 1968, locates the beginning of anthropology in the Enlightenment. According to him, the notion of cultural determinism, or the realization that people acquired customs that existed outside their biogenetic makeup, existed in the 18th century; it was this realization of cultural determinism which marked the beginning of anthropology. He rejects Hodgen's view as an example of the idealistic orientation of the Treggert school of historical interpretation.

Hodgen calls attention to the importance of the Greek historian, Herodotus. Herodotus, she says, was not only an ethnographer who described customs carefully; he was also an ethnologist who compared customs.

As I have noted earlier, description and comparison are not sufficient to define the distinctiveness of anthropology. The ancient Persians were in many ways cultural relativists; Darius the Persian emperor tolerated cultural pluralism. Other groups were also sensitive to cultural differences. The Hindu caste system, for example, promoted and sustained cultural differences. What was missing from all of these exercises in cross-cultural awareness was the key element of the "anthropological vision," namely, a self-conscious attempt to understand the nature of humanity through the understanding of other people. The diversity of others was noted, perhaps used for humorous commentary; but no further use was made of the data of otherness.

Hodgen notes that from the time of Herodotus onwards, there seems to have been a preoccupation in the West with the description of abnormal humans and customs, for such treatises increase and are quite common by the first century A.D. This fascination with abnormal human shapes and customs received an impetus in the 13th century when several authors produced volumes compiling the accumulated corpus of knowledge on such topics. Collections of artifacts or cultural curios continued as an important aspect of Western tradition.

Hodgen points out that the Renaissance differed from the medieval period in its attempt to explain these observed differences in customs. One explanatory model was degenerationism, the belief that abnormal humans had once been normal but had lost the good and natural customs. The discovery of the New World and the existence of human customs very different from those of the Europeans posed a cognitive problem of how to interpret or place the New World humans. In the late Renaissance it was not uncommon for Indians to be exhibited as a different type of human; on occasion, Indians, sub-Saharan Africans, apes and monkeys were exhibited together to demonstrate their affinity. The idea of explaining non-Western others, using the symbol of the savage (the wild non-West as opposed to the orderly West), gained currency, and the New World inhabitants and sub-Saharan Africans were lumped as savages and located in the Great Chain of Being, the hierarchic taxonomic model of Christian cosmology, as sub-humans, under humans and above beasts.

According to Hodgen, then, modern anthropology is a 20th-century version of medieval taxonomy; its distinctive task is to complete the grand scheme of the Great Chain. This medieval concept of the Great Chain of Being has been coupled with the Greco-Roman principle of change. Thus what we have today is temporalized taxonomy as opposed to the spatial taxonomy of the church period.

Marvin Harris rejects Hodgen's interpretation of the history of anthropology. According to him, it is not the collection of odd facts to flesh out the Great Chain which marks anthropology's distinctive contribution but the development of a scientific study of culture. Anthropology's beginnings, therefore, must be traced to the 18th century when scholars began to discuss cultural determinants of human behavior, and to discuss the mechanistic laws which guided these determinants.

According to Harris, the epistemology of John Locke provided the foundation for the emergence of the science of culture. Harris cites the writings of many French and Scottish scholars who reflected Locke's epistemology, and argues that the majority of 18th-century scholars believed in the power of enculturation or socialization as the shaper of human nature and behavior. This, according to Harris, was a radical belief which distinguished the 18th century not only from earlier centuries but from later centuries as well. The emphasis on the importance of culture rather than biology led to the emergence of the "literal as well as socialist tradition of class and racial democracy." (Harris 1968:15)

When 18th-century scholars propounded the doctrine of the "psychic unity of mankind," says Harris, they believed that hereditary differences did not cause cultural differences; differences among diverse others were due to differences in experience and the opportunity to use reason. The thinkers of the Enlightenment promoted tolerance of alien customs, at the same time upholding the "rational" institutions of the 18th century as ideal. Their orientation should not be confused with the "cultural relativism" which is promoted by modern anthropologists.

To quote Harris (1968:13):

> Perhaps the reason why anthropologists have been reluctant to trace the culture concept to Locke's *Essay* is that Locke, in company with all of the 18th century's formal and de facto students of culture, despite the power they attributed to experience to shape customs and beliefs, did not abandon the notion that there were universally valid moral beliefs and right and wrong rules and modes of conduct. It was not the concept of culture that was absent in 1750, but rather the moral indifference of cultural relativism...social science followed Locke in his conviction

that despite differences in experience, reason — correctly applied, led man everywhere to the same social institutions, moral beliefs and scientific technical truths.

The search for the laws of cultural determinants of behavior is, of course, an aspect of anthropology. But Harris' analysis does not suggest what distinguishes anthropology from other social science disciplines. The Renaissance thinker was also concerned with the nature of enculturation, although he did not phrase his concern in the same manner as Enlightenment thinkers and was not entirely free from religious interpretations. The view that the physical as well as biological universe was governed by mechanical laws emerged during the late Renaissance, in particular the 17th century; but because of the reluctance by many Reniassance scholars to incorporate humans in this worldview, Harris lays the beginning of a science of anthropology (as a "nomothetic" or generalizing science applied to man) in the lap of the Enlightenment. I would argue, however, that many scholars of the Renaissance undertook comparative studies in myths and customs from a naturalistic and rationalistic perspective which was no different from that of scholars of the 18th century. Hodgen (1964:270), for example, points out that scholars such as Niccolo Machiavelli (1469-1527), Louis Le Roy (c. 1510-1677), and Jean Badin (1530-1596) "were empiricists as well as secularists. They sought to avoid all the pitfalls of other Renaissance scholars, who still working under the shadow of scholasticism, were without experience in the day-to-day affairs of human communities. Instead of relying on a tradition which cast men's destiny in a wholly pessimistic mold, they advocated a return to the record of human experience as found in the several histories of the several nations." Many compared the customs of the European past (the ancestral human other) and the non-Western present (the ethnographic other) to understand the nature of humankind.

The following quotes from Montaigne (1533-1592) provide some examples of a Renaissance thinker's awareness of cultural causality and cultural relativity:

> How the ideas of men diverge!
>
> There is nothing in which the world varies so much as in customs and laws. Many a thing is abominable here that is commended elsewhere.
>
> Not only every country, but every city and every profession has its particular form of civility.
>
> In short, every nation has many habits and customs which to any other nation are not only strange but amazing and barbarous!

Having argued that neither the studies which stress anthropology's preoccupation with abnormal customs to flesh out the taxonomy of divine or developmental creation nor those which emphasize its scientific study of cultural influences have succeeded in pinpointing the distinctiveness of anthropology, I will now present my arguments for locating the origin of anthropology in the Renaissance.

It is important to keep in mind during the following discussion that what we call the "Renaissance" is our construct. We compartmentalize the past into different epochs as a convenient way of talking about major shifts in cognitive orientation. The changes themselves occur gradually, and at any one time different worldviews may coexist, and scholars may use different paradigms. We identify certain writers as representative of an epoch, which itself is a construct which symbolizes a certain worldview. (This is comparable to an ethnographer choosing a key informant or major individual by means of whom he talks about a society.)

As noted in the previous section, many late Renaissance thinkers were rationalists, not different from many thinkers of the so-called "Enlightenment" period, and in fact not all that different from the Scholastics of the Medieval Period except that, in the Enlightenment thinkers' emphasis on reason and rationality they left out the divinity referred to in previous epochs. (The Enlightenment thinker in his discussion of divinity was concerned with the origin and function of "natural religion" as opposed to the scholars of earlier periods who, when they discussed divinity, were concerned with the historical Christian god.) The Enlightenment thinkers looked back at the events which occurred during the Renaissance, in particular the religious persecutions and religious expressions of various kinds, and concluded that religion was irrational and should be excluded from all legitimate concerns of inquiry about the laws of human nature. For them, prophetic religions did not reveal truth. Enlightenment rationalism, although it was a cultural continuation of medieval scholars' preoccupation with the divine reason which lay behind the workings of the universe, was presented as a substitute for theological dogmatism, which to many Enlightenment thinkers was linked with irrationalism and its social consequences. The scholars of the Enlightenment were attempting to evolve a model of reason as a practical, pragmatic, utilitarian model of reality which to them would serve the needs of mankind. The universalism of the Enlightenment thinker was a universalism of rationality which transcended the parochial, emotional sensibilities of particular nations. The Enlightenment thinker saw science as an expression of this universal rationality.

Elements of modern anthropology may be traced to Greco-Roman and Scholastic periods, anthropology's nomothetic thinking to the Enlightenment, the phenomenological emphasis on fieldwork and participant observation to the Romantic period. The aspect of anthropology with which I am most concerned, however, and the one which I feel is primary, is its enterprise of making use of the non-Western other to define what it means to be human, and for this aspect we must go to the Renaissance.

In his paper titled "The Renaissance Foundations of Anthropology," John Rowe (1965:1-20) describes a tradition of explaining cultural differences which he says began in the Renaissance of the 14th and 15th centuries.

For the Renaissance scholar, cultural differences were important because they provided insight into the nature of humankind. Initially, Renaissance scholars sought an understanding of humanness by comparing classical antiquity with their own times. According to Rowe, "Renaissance studies of classical antiquity not only stimulated a general interest in differences among men, they also provided models for describing such differences."

Rowe points out: "The essence of the anthropological point of view is that in order to understand ourselves we need to study others. In contrast, the ancient Greeks for the most part held that the way to understand ourselves is to study ourselves, while what others do is irrelevant."

Eric Wolf also notes modern anthropology's connection with the Renaissance (1964:10): "Indeed, latter-day anthropology has brought to fruition an undertaking begun by the Renaissance, which rediscovered the worlds of the Greeks and Romans and rendered these worlds contemporary in the process of rediscovery."

Margaret Hodgen sees the continuity of anthropological ideas from Greco-Roman times to the present; but as indicated by the title of her book, *Early Anthropology in the Sixteenth and Seventeenth Centuries,* she emphasizes the importance of the late Renaissance in fostering the emergence of modern anthropology and other comparative disciplines. To quote Hodgen (1964:8):

> This sixteenth- and seventeenth-century literature, which laid the foundation of modern anthropology, comparative religions, anthropogeography, and many other related studies, exhibits the emergence of what must now be regarded as scientific method in the study of culture and society: first, in a definite transition from the motive of entertainment to that of organized inquiry; second, in the more or less clear statement of questions or problems of importance; and third, in the choice of organizing ideas to be employed in dealing with the problem of the origin of man, the diversity of cultures, the significance of similarities, the sequence of high civilizations, and the course of the process of cultural change.

Fred Voget (1975:20-21) also recognizes the importance of the Renaissance for the emergence of anthropology as a discipline, but observes that a true discipline of anthropology could not emerge during the Renaissance because of the theological authority which dominated this period:

> A number of special developments in the course of Western civilization conspired to make the Renaissance a prophetic moment in the rise of a science of man. First, there was the stimulus conveyed by a renewal of contacts with Greco-Roman humanism and science. Second, the Renaissance witnessed the rise of a scientific orientation and the accomplishment of scientific proofs that gave scholars a sense of importance and of confidence in their own discoveries. Third, voyages of discovery followed by conquest and settlement brought a vast new world to light, un-

known to the ancients and not even alluded to in Christian traditions
present during the Renaissance that militated against an objective investigation of mankind. There was, first, the hard strength of the Christian tradition, which narrowed interpretation and problem definition to
Christian history.

In contrast with Voget, *I would argue that the Judeo-Christian tradition,
far from strangling an incipient anthropology, in fact gave legitimacy to the
studies which compared the other and us.* For anthropology to be sustained,
a naturalistic perspective in and of itself is insufficient; there must exist an
added principle within the cultural structure which renders legitimate or
valid the comparison of the known human with the unknown human, in
terms of what is culturally held to be true and untrue and to unite these two
in developing a model of human integration.

The Study of the History of Anthropology as a
Sub-Discipline of Anthropology

The "history" of anthropology is not a single history but many, depending on the perspective adopted by the interpreter of the past. Both professional historians and professional anthropologists have attempted the task,
each armed with their own batteries of technique and professional reference
points. The histories differ in philosophy and method. Some emphasize the
continuity of certain ideas (Hodgen 1964), others the coexistence of com-
peting models, or the emergence of dominant models during a particular
period (Lowie 1938; Honigmann 1976; Malefijt 1974; Voget 1975). Some
provide biographical gossip (Hays 1958; Silverman 1981; Kardiner and
Preble 1963), whereas others explore the philosophical biases of individual
anthropologists (Harris 1968; Hatch 1973; Leaf 1979). Yet others have
enumerated the facts related to the establishment of various anthropological bureaus and associations, and the controversies surrounding their establishment (Hinsley 1981). In some, scholars have provided descriptions of
the social milieu in which a certain school of anthropology was popular,
and the context of national traditions in which certain anthropological
schools of thought emerged (Wolf 1964; Stocking, Jr. 1968, 1974; Thoresen
1975; Diamond 1980). Some devote attention to the history of the sub-
disciplines of anthropology, emphasizing the distinctiveness of linguistic
anthropology, archaeological anthropology, and physical anthropology
(Brew 1968). There are also a few historical readers or collections of the
writings of prominent anthropologists (Slotkin 1965; Bohannon and Glazer
1973; Darnell 1974). And Columbia University Press has published in the
past decade several separate volumes on the contributions of particular
anthropologists such as Ruth Benedict, Ralph Linton and Robert Lowie.
The *Newsletter of the History of Anthropology* periodically publishes

information on doctoral dissertations and other research on the history of anthropology.

In a report on a conference on the history of anthropology sponsored by the Social Science Research Council, Hymes (1962) noted that anthropology should be studied in the same way that anthropologists would study cultural traditions, and presented the view that "we must prepare to train some anthropologists as specialists in the history of anthropology."

Recently the sub-discipline of the history of anthropology has become prominent within the discipline of anthropology. See, for example, the book *Observers Observed,* edited by Stocking, Jr. (1983). The following paragraphs review some of these works and comment upon the significance of the fact that library research on the history of anthropology has now become an acceptable substitute for fieldwork. I suggest that this interest in the history of the discipline is a process by which anthropologists are demythologizing the human other. Through scholarship which examines the personal and cultural biases of those who wrote about human others, and by analyzing the interpersonal and institutional conflicts of the periods in which human others were described, several studies have provided an understanding of the anthropologists and the periods of the Western tradition when it was logical to view the human others in a certain manner (see the *Newsletter of the History of Anthropology*).

The two institutions which have led in this trend are the University of California at Berkeley and the University of Pennsylvania. The following paragraphs review some of these developments.

George Stocking, Jr., a historian of anthropology, who is currently at the University of Chicago, has influenced many anthropologists writing on the history of anthropology. The intellectual debt which is owed to him is acknowledged by Elvin Hatch and Regna Darnell, two anthropologists who have engaged in research on the history of anthropology. In 1973 Hatch published a highly readable book on the history of anthropology which examined differences in monistic and dualistic assumptions of the nature of cultural creation and maintenance. In 1974 Darnell edited a useful collection of essays on the history of anthropology using a sociology of knowledge approach. Curtis M. Hinsley, an historian who believes that the history of anthropology "should not be left to anthropologists" to study, also acknowledges his intellectual debt to Stocking in his 1981 book on the history of American anthropology from 1846 to 1910. Stocking has also been responsible for the publication of the correspondence and selected writings of Franz Boas, and the reissue of the writings of the 19th-century physical anthropologist James Cowles Pritchard who anticipated most of Darwin's ideas on evolution.

Regna Darnell is unusual in that she earned her Ph.D. in a department of anthropology for writing her dissertation on the history of anthropology. She has acknowledged that she was influenced by the teaching and writings of Irving Hallowell, Loren Eiseley and Dell Hymes and says, "I was fortunate to acquire at the University of Pennsylvania a broad interdisciplinary background for [the study of the history of anthropology]. My dissertation on the history of American anthropology from 1890 to 1920 is still virtually unique as an acceptable topic for a Ph.D. degree in cultural anthropology. I was strongly encouraged by my major advisor, Dell Hymes to believe that I could be an anthropologist without doing fieldwork for my dissertation. Although I have since done considerable fieldwork, I still do not see it as the only route to professional identity as an anthropologist."

Darnell's statement that she was "strongly encouraged" by her advisor "to believe that I could be an anthropologist without doing fieldwork for my dissertation" is, in my view, very significant as it shows the acceptance of the study of the history of anthropology as a sub-discipline. Lists of recent American doctoral dissertations in anthropology which are based on library research are published regularly in the *Newsletter of the History of Anthropology*.

This increased concern with the history of anthropology represents an attempt to find the meaning of anthropology. I suggest that this may represent a revitalistic movement in anthropology, an attempt to understand the rationalizations that support the study of the human other. Historical scholarship on the discipline of anthropology has converged with anthropological scholarship on the history of anthropology. In my view this is bound to have some positive consequences in producing what may be identified as "authentic anthropology," which I discuss in Chapter Twelve.

Chapter Eleven

Anthropology in the Humanities

Interpretation of the Human Other

As Clifford Geertz (1973:14) notes, an aim of anthropology is "the enlargement of the universe of human discourse." Using a semiotic approach, Geertz says that

> ...anthropological writings are themselves interpretations, and second and third order ones to boot. (By definition, only a "native" makes first order ones: it's his culture.) They are, thus, fictions: fictions, in the sense that they are "something made," "something fashioned" — the original meaning *fictio* — not that they are false, unfactual, or merely "as if" thought experiments. (Geertz 1973:15)

During the past 400 years anthropological descriptions have been viewed mistakenly by many as objective data. Based on the assumption that the data are objective, misleading and erroneous statements have been made about human nature and about "racial" and cultural differences. The fallacy of reification has been a part of anthropology. While the process of reification is itself a viable cultural orientation, it has no place in scientific method; and yet anthropological inventions — the concepts, definitions and other abstract generalizations of the discipline — have been accepted as physical realities, in part because of the view of anthropology as a natural or social science. Anthropologists, for the most part, collect as data the conceptual realities of other peoples that are causal-functionally and symbolically interconnected in distinctive ways, and then themselves impose a particular conceptual schema to approximate the causal-functional and symbolic interconnections invented by the "natives."

The conception of anthropology as a science has promoted racism and ethnocentrism rather than combatting them, as anthropology claims to do. It is possible, as Geertz suggests (1971), that anthropology's ideological commitment to the view of itself as a natural or social science stems from the fallacious conception of the "Sciences [as] being masculine and the

110

Humanities [as] being feminine" and the belief that anthropology's contributions will not be recognized unless they are presented as scientific discoveries or explanations.

Science and the Humanities

In order to illuminate why the profession of anthropology sometimes seems to lack understanding of its objectives and scope, it is important to unravel some of the confusing statements made about whether anthropology is a "science" or one of the "humanities." Academic institutions differ in whether they categorize anthropology as a natural science, a social science, or as part of the humanities. It is possible that anthropology's significance as a perspective to promote discourse, incorporating the human other, is blurred because of the needs of anthropologists affiliated with academic anthropology.

Dell Hymes (1969) argues that the malaise of contemporary anthropology derives from its being rooted in academic departments. The practitioners of anthropology in academic departments are under pressure to seek grants, to publish, to define their identity as scientists. Often they engage in trivial research, justified in the name of science, and defend their academic existence using the rhetoric of scientism. Also, their respectability within the academic context and their ability to function as consultants for monetary rewards outside the academia are linked with their identity as scientists. Thus it is easy for academic anthropologists to forget the humanistic roots and scope of anthropology.

A confusion exists in Western thought concerning the relationship between science and the humanities. They are often portrayed as parallel, equivalent and often antagonistic structures, as in C.P. Snow's discussion of the "two cultures."

In a general sense, all human activities have a scientific dimension. All human beings must use the scientific method to survive, a method which involves the development and testing of models which approximate reality so that regularities and the relationships of phenomena may be known and reality made more predictable. Narrowly defined, "disciplinary" science constitutes a rigorous set of empirical studies and controlled experiments (which should be verifiable by independent observers) in which various hypotheses are tested to derive the laws of nature. Broadly defined, however, any self-conscious attempt to understand physical or *conceptual* realities is scientific. Humanistic scholarship incorporates science in its dedication to the verification of facts; interpretations of relationships that could be causal or nomothetic are no less scientific than are the theoretical explanations of causal, functional relationships. However, differences arise in how the facts are presented to convey meaning. In this sense, the humanities are rooted in mythological, symbolic discourse.

Science is method; it does not in itself have any meaning. Science is the process by which an organism builds up a model of nature. Nature is not human-centered; the laws of nature are not willed by humans. The human concerns of intentionality, motivation and meaning cannot be explained or grasped by the scientific method; these are the subject of the humanities. Be they theology, history, philosophy, literature or anthropology, the humanities interpret and use the findings of science to derive meaning as it is relevant to a particular society at a particular time. The often mentioned criticism of science come from a misunderstanding and misuse of scientific data. If, as some critics of science have said, science and the "scientific worldview" have failed, it is because the humanities have failed.

Religion, philosophy, literature, history, the classics, and anthropology are all humanities in the sense that they are involved in helping people conceptualize their experience and scientific knowledge in a meaningful way. A computer or a TV set are not the enemies of man, with evil mechanistic intentions, out to deprave the mind of youth; they simply are. Whether they are "evil" depends on the uses to which they are put, the meanings imputed to them. Science cannot "fail," but the humanities can fail to interpret science in a meaningful way. Science is atomistic and analytic; the humanities are holistic and synthetic. The value of humanistic scholarship is its being able to use science and at the same time be sensitive to human concerns and the consequences of human inventions, material or otherwise.

Anthropology, as part of the humanities, must examine its inventions of the human other. Why is the human other a necessary component to understand the nature of humankind? Why are the human others invented in a certain manner? What are the consequences of anthropological inventions?

In order for an anthropologist to function as what I would call an authentic anthropologist, he or she must study the cultural tradition in which the anthropological inventions are used. Anthropologists must study the needs and concerns of their society to interpret why their inventions make sense to their audience, how and why their inventions fit in their society. Above all, anthropology must address the following question: what is the meaning of discourse on the human other in the Western tradition? The study of the history of anthropology must serve as a key to such an understanding. I suggest that the study of the history of anthropology must be the organizing principle or theme in the teaching of anthropology and that it is necessary to initiate students into anthropology with a course on how anthropology functions in the Western tradition.

Anthropologists make use of the scientific method. Biological anthropologists, ecological anthropologists, medical anthropologists, and so on, all make use of scientific techniques; but those who stop at the definition of themselves as hard-nosed scientists miss the point of their anthropological contribution. It is not the collection of data which makes their contribution distinctively anthropological but the way the data are used. The human other is a source of data, but the data become intelligible, relevant and meaningful in the process of defining what it means to be human, i.e., in the formulations of the models of human integration. Anthropology examines the human other to interpret the totality of human possibility and experience.

It may be argued that a primary concern of anthropology is to investigate regularities in human behavior, recurrence of institutional types and the laws that govern human body, mind and culture, and thus that anthropology is primarily a nomothetic science and not a historical, particularistic discourse. My own view is that if the scientific component of anthropology is separated and made into a rationalization for maintaining anthropology as a scientific discipline, this will result in anthropology's losing its objectives and scope: physical anthropology will become part of biology, cultural anthropology will be differentiated into comparative sociology, comparative psychology and comparative linguistics, and archaeology will become part of history.

Science and the Sociopolitical Context

Science does not exist and develop in a cultural vacuum. The availability of funds for particular kinds of scientific research and the socio-political climate shape the questions which scientists ask, and promote or minimize the use of certain scientific discoveries. I have already discussed the context in which anthropology developed and how it diversified into different orientations in different national-political contexts (Chapters Two and Ten). An investigation of the nature of disciplines and their linkages to social and cultural factors must not be construed as a rejection of the validity of the disciplines. As a matter of fact, as Gould (1981) correctly notes, such an investigation helps to eliminate bad or vulgar science, reduce the misuse of science, and promote or enhance the significant contributions of science.

In a recent book called *Science, Ideology and World View* (1981), John Greene develops Thomas Kuhn's seminal contribution to the study of the history of science. Kuhn (1962), in *The Structure of Scientific Revolutions,* points out that the common assumption of scientific knowledge as a lineal progression of eliminating error is erroneous. Scientific knowledge is predicated upon the effectiveness of the dominant paradigm to answer questions. A paradigm is a model of scientific inquiry, a way of explaining phenomena. It defines the legitimate problems for a discipline, and methods of research. But gradually, as hypotheses are tested, anomalous data crop up, results that are not expected. Ptolemaic astronomy, for example, was predicated on the assumption that heavenly bodies moved around the earth on crystalline spheres. The number of spheres required to explain the erratic movements of the planets became so numerous that the Copernican "revolution" was assured by virtue of its explanatory effectiveness. Scientific paradigms, from Kuhn's point of view, have a distinctive internal logic which dominates research questions and answers; but when they fail to provide satisfying answers, they are replaced by paradigms which do. Evolutionary anthropology had an internal logic which made sense in the Western tradition. See Nancy Stepan (1981) for a detailed discussion of this internal logic and the relationship between the logic of evolutionism and the socio-political context of the 19th century.

Greene argues that the history of science is a transformational process. The emergence of new paradigms reflects shifts in worldview and ideology. How a society conceives of nature and life, what its social and political ideologies are, play an important role in shaping scientific paradigms. There exists a dialectical relationship between science and its socio-political context, and a "symbiosis between thought and society."

As an example, Greene discusses the paradigm of "natural selection" which Charles Darwin systematically formulated and presented in 1859. Although anthropological views of evolutionism did not develop from Darwin's views, the Darwinian model provided a powerful prop for the evolutionary anthropology of the late 19th and early 20th centuries. In most historical versions of Darwin's contribution, the concept of natural selection is presented as a naturalistic explanation of life triumphing over a religious explanation; and this biological theory is then thought of as having provided a justification for competition in social, political and economic realism (hence such terms as "Social Darwinism"). However, Greene argues that rather than determining socio-political philosophy of the 19th century, Darwin's theory is itself a byproduct of distinctively British theories of political economy which subscribed to self-regulatory principles in the market place and related notions of competition, struggle for survival, and survival of the fittest. (Greene, incidentally, does not mention an interesting fact which supports his interpretation: when Darwin's book appeared, Karl Marx wrote to Friedrich Engels that Darwin had projected the operating principles of 19th-century British political economy and social policy onto the animal kingdom.)

Although the above formulations are quite valid, it must be noted that the socially determined knowledge systems become historically evolved vehicles for the conception of reality by people of subsequent generations. In other words, the Darwinian model became a metaphor; the researchers who followed Darwin investigated the adaptive processes with the symbol of natural selection, which combined propositions about variability, fertility and mortality, and the survival of the fittest. As Geertz (1973) points out, "The sociology of knowledge ought to be called the sociology of meaning, for what is socially determined is not the nature of conception but

the vehicles of conception.'' Therefore, in discussing the origin and maintenance of modern anthropology or any other discipline, it is necessary to
investigate the historically evolved symbols or metaphors which the scholars
use in conceptualizing physical, biological, social, cultural or psychological
phenomena.

Within anthropology, the ancient organic analogue, or the metaphor of
the organism, was revived in the 19th century and for a long time has been
important in conceptualizing social structure and function, and
social/cultural change and development. Prior to that, Newtonian physics
provided the metaphor of the machine to conceptualize human society and
behavior. The Great Chain metaphor of the Church fathers has continued
to be important for taxonomy. The language analogue, with its reference to
communication and information, has become popular in contemporary
anthropology. In considering the metaphors that aid our understanding of
humankind, we must also examine the distinctive feature of modern
anthropology, viz., its use of the human other. The discourse on human
others, as I have suggested, has a mythological or symbolic function within
the Western tradition. The study of this function is within the scope of the
humanities.

Anthropology, History and the Anthropology of History

Anthropologists, as interpreters of data on human others, can be compared to historians in their efforts to make the interpretations meaningful in
relation to the intellectual concerns and anxieties of a particular period.
Richard Schlatter, in his introduction to Eric Wolf's (1964) book titled
Anthropology, points out,

> [The anthropologist] must sift the whole of man's culture again and
> again, reassessing, reinterpreting, rediscovering, translating into a
> modern idiom, making available the materials and the blueprints with
> which his contemporaries can build their own culture, bringing to the
> center of the stage that which a past generation has judged irrelevant
> but which is now again usable, sending into the storage that which has
> become, for the moment, too familiar and too habitual to stir our
> imagination, preserving it for a posterity to which it will once more seem
> fresh.

Because of the perception of history as narrative description of the past,
or as speculations about reasons for the rise and fall of civilization, and
because of the reaction against certain versions of historicism or historical
determinism in favor of cultural determinism, anthropologists who are
committed to empirical research have difficulty in perceiving the close
affinity between anthropology and history (cf. Evans-Pritchard 1961). The
British anthropologist A.R. Radcliffe-Brown advocated synchronic analysis
of simple societies because he believed that historical reconstruction would

be at best conjectural in the absence of written records. He made a distinction between social anthropology which was the study of structure and function, and ethnology which he defined as a historical discipline concerned with racial and cultural history (see Chapter Two). The mental-structural determinism of Claude Levi-Strauss is a-historical in its orientation, dealing with "a-historical" peoples.

History and anthropology, however, have much in common. As Robert Anderson (1967) points out in his paper, "The Flirtation of Anthropology and History,"

> It seems both desirable and feasible that anthropology and history should permit their intellectual territories to overlap and thus form a common intermediate area in which each would profit from collaboration with the other. Such collaboration is called for because the two disciplines, each in its own territory, have for some time now been devoted to the same basic pursuits.

Bernard Cohn (1980) in his paper, "History and Anthropology: The State of Play," points out correctly that both history and anthropology "share a great deal at the epistemological level." History deals primarily with the study of people who are distant in time, and anthropology with the study of people who are distant in space (cf. Chapter Nine).

Anthropologists deal with the human others who are relevant to their society. The anthropologist is selective in the use of the human other, and his/her interpretations are meant for the West of a particular time; the human other will be reinterpreted at different times. Certain human others have greater significance in the West, and their significance changes depending on what a particular generation is looking for. Some anthropologists can write highly imaginative ethnographies that become evocative representations in the West.

The historian, too, is selective in his use of the past. As Collingwood has noted, history deals with "a past which in some sense is still living in the present." The historian provides interpretive judgments about the past which are open to reinterpretations and re-evaluations. Certain periods of the past may have greater significance than others, and certain events of the past can become crystallized as evocative symbolic representations in the hands of imaginative historians.

Both historians and anthropologists have emphasized the significance of the concept of culture (Ware 1940) and some historians view history as "retrospective cultural anthropology" (Hughes 1964). In the 20th century, both disciplines have had frequent internal debates about the objectivity of "facts," about the validity of positivistic, generalizing orientations, and about the significance of idealistic, particularistic orientations.

Within American anthropology there has been a longstanding feud between generalists, who sought to discover the laws or regularities of cultural development, and particularists who sought to describe cultural histories. In 1935, Alfred Kroeber, the "dean" of American anthropology for several decades, tried to resolve this American dilemma by suggesting that "...there is a historical attitude and approach as well as a scientific attitude and approach, and that, in a field like anthropology, each has its genuine problems and equally important and fruitful results." (Kroeber 1935:566) Kroeber identified himself as half humanist and half scientist. It is not uncommon for anthropologists to hold that anthropology is a discipline which is in the natural and social sciences as well as in the humanities (Wolf 1964), and the same is true for history (Carr 1961).

I believe that it is the humanist component which provides anthropology and history with their holistic philosophy, relevance and meaning, and therefore it is ideal to start a beginning student in anthropology with an historical discussion of how and why anthropology is an intelligent, coherent mode of human discourse in his/her cultural tradition.

In 1966 William Sturtevant saw in ethnohistory an opportunity to integrate the theory and methods of anthropology and history. The approach called ethnohistory offers a way to bring together the contributions of anthropologists and historians, and to forge a new orientation in historical anthropology. Marshall Sahlins (1983) has called this new orientation the *Anthropology of History*. Others, however, have voiced concern about the difficulty of achieving adequate competency in two different fields (Hudson 1973).

Ethnohistory has been defined in different ways, but since the mid-20th century it has generally been understood to mean the anthropological study of the past of non-literate, i.e., non-Western, peoples by using documentary or material evidence such as written and/or archaeological records. Ethnohistory is distinguished from "folk" history, which refers to the peoples' conceptions of their past, and from "oral" history, although anthropologists have usually combined the three in writing ethnographies. The cultural anthropologists of the United States in particular have sought to understand the continuities and changes in different cultural traditions, the historic contacts between different groups, the structural patterns of earlier periods, as well as the cognitive and emotional orientations revealed in peoples' conceptions of their past.

It may be that such a combination is a more fruitful mode of inquiry than restricting anthropological research to structural analysis at the synchronic level in order to discover abstract, general principles of relationships. As Sahlins (1983) has pointed out, anthropologists undertake the study of concrete events, as do historians, as well as contribute to a cross-cultural and historical understanding of the different concepts of history. A unified approach to ethnohistory which includes folk and oral histories can develop into an important orientation called "the anthropology of history" which can further the scope of anthropology.

Historians do not confine their research to the diachronic analysis of particulars; the structures of the past as well as developmental sequences have been studied, in combination, by historians. Many have also studied the peoples' conceptions of their past, and the images, metaphors, myths and symbols used in the conceptions of other peoples. The image of the human other in the Western tradition has been investigated by historians for several decades. Historians have examined specific semantic structures as they were used in the West to identify the human others, and have described the Western images of the non-Western peoples that tell us about the cognitive and emotional orientations of the West. These studies have provided many insights into the problem dealt with in his book. (See, for example, Curtin 1964; Chiapelli 1976; Dawson 1967; Baudet 1965; Berkhofer 1978, 1979; Honour 1977; Dudley and Novak 1972).

These developments in anthropology and history have the potential to promote a greater understanding of the mental processes as well as the politico-economic contexts conducive for the emergence of certain structures of thought, and will enhance our humanistic discourse not only on particular cultural traditions but on the structures of global history.

The Need to Teach an Introductory Course in Anthropology as Part of the Humanities

Anthropology presents a paradox. It is a discipline that transcends the parochial biases of particular societies and periods; and yet it often serves to legitimize parochial biases. An analysis of this paradox involves the philosophical, historical and anthropological study of the Western tradition in which modern anthropology evolved and in which it is, at the epistemological level, rooted.

I believe that a philosophical, anthropological and historical understanding of the role of anthropology ought to be a necessary aspect of undergraduate curriculum in anthropology. In order to illustrate this point, I will finish this chapter with a short essay concerning the role of anthropology which I wrote (under the title "Anthropology in the Humanities") for the March 1984 issue of the American Anthropological Association's *Newsletter*.

> In educational curricula in the United States, anthropology is usually listed as a social science and/or natural science. Despite the fact that anthropologists qualify for funding from agencies such as the National Endowment for the Humanities, and despite the existence of societies and journals committed to humanistic anthropology, we do not have a clearly formulated view of how anthropology fits in the academic domain identified as the humanities in most universities and colleges.
>
> The implications and consequences of not explicitly identifying the humanistic side of anthropology in the academia are multifold. Beginning

students are often unable to grasp the philosophy of holism and the meaning of anthropological discourse, and anthropology is often left out from the humanistic course requirements of the General Education Programs of the universities and colleges, which reduces the ability of anthropology departments to function as viable academic units with sufficient enrollment.

Many scholars have called attention to the fact that increased specialization has resulted in anthropology losing its vision as the study of humankind; in many instances, discourse among the various specialists is almost impossible. Some anthropologists have actively proposed moving away from anthropology's traditional disciplinary and conceptual unity. Leslie White promoted the creation of a separate discipline called culturology, or the science of culture. In 1981 in the *Anthropology Newsletter,* John Messenger argued that "Since increased specialization has all but shattered the traditional holism of anthropology, why not let physical anthropology join biology, archaeology join history, anthropological linguistics join linguistics, and cultural anthropology join sociology?"

It appears to me that the disciplinary and conceptual unity of anthropology derives from its humanistic principle that enables us to comprehend the meaning of anthropological scholarship. The data and theories produced by different branches of anthropology promote certain types of discourse that might be counter-productive and misleading unless anthropologists are willing to bring a philosopher's logical, critical inquiry and a historian's sensitivity to evaluate and interpret the sociocultural contexts in which scientific knowledge is accepted as relevant. Data may be produced by the scientific method, but it is the humanist who analyzes the data in relation to the quality and value of human life, and anthropologists, in my view, must engage in this type of humanistic discourse that transcends the parochial concerns of specialized research. The strength of anthropology as a unified study of humankind lies in its synthesizing human knowledge, particularly the use of knowledge on other peoples.

Today we recognize readily the fact that anthropology responds to the concerns and needs of a generation, and we are not afraid to discuss the fact that the founding fathers of anthropology were in fact reflecting the prevailing biases of the period. We, of this generation, are no different in this regard; we participate in the structures of meaning of our culture and therefore must ask the question of why and how the data on other people are meaningful to us. The anthropologist, as a humanist, must examine the implications and validity of the various scientific data and formulations of different branches of anthropology in order to promote human discourse rather than invoking the flag of neutrality and letting half-baked theories and biased data become myths that serve the needs of particular groups.

The emergence of the study of the history of anthropology as a sub-discipline in the past two decades, through the writings of scholars such as the late Irving Hallowell and Loren Eiseley, as well as Dell Hymes, George Stocking, Jr., Regna Darnell, Eric Wolf, Murray Leaf, Elvin Hatch, Jacob Gruber, Fred Voget, and Stanley Diamond, provide us with an opportunity and an avenue for maintaining anthropology as a unified discipline and at the same time being aware of the pitfalls and dangers of making "scientific" pronouncements that are proved to be wrong by succeeding generations. This kind of scholarship also brings us closer to historians and philosophers who have in recent times examined the anthropological theories and the various Western images of non-Western peoples of different times, and firmly places anthropology in the humanities.

In this regard, I wish to follow up on some thoughts I expressed in the November 1982 issue of the *Anthropology Newsletter* regarding a new course, "Non-Western Cultures in the Western Tradition," which I proposed for inclusion in the General Education Program at California State University, Fullerton. I suggested at that time that as part of the humanities requirement of the General Education Program, it could "make an important and relevant contribution to an understanding of both anthropology and Western civilization" and that it could "play a significant role in education, affecting the role which anthropology plays in the general education curriculum and its viability as an academic department through increased enrollment." In 1983, the student response to the course was overwhelmingly positive, with very high enrollments in all sections of the class.

The main objectives of the course are to examine how and why data on non-Western people were and are used in the Western intellectual tradition and how this use of data became identified as anthropological inquiry; to introduce the beginning student to the fact that the nature of anthropological theories cannot be grasped without understanding the nature of the relationship between the West and non-Western peoples; and to investigate the cultural structures of the West that are conducive to the use of other peoples in theorizing about the nature of humankind. In other words, the course concerns the origins and function of post-16th-century anthropology as an aspect of the Western intellectual tradition.

I believe that an introductory course on "Anthropology and the Western Tradition" can combine anthropological, philosophical and historical concerns, a combination that could strengthen the discipline's unified structure and contribution and at the same time help anthropology departments expand in enrollments with a course of that kind taught as part of the humanities in the General Education Program.

Chapter Twelve

Toward an Authentic Anthropology

> Those who cannot remember the past are condemned to repeat it.
> —Santayana, *The Life of Reason*
> Vol. I, *Reason in Common Sense.*

In an article titled "The Anthropology of Authenticity: Everyman His Own Anthropologist," David Kaplan (1974) attacked those anthropologists who, according to him, advocated the re-inventing or rediscovering of anthropology. Such anthropologists, he said, propagated a "voluntaristic existential brand of radicalism with its emphasis on subjectivity, consciousness, praxis, and the search for the authentic self."

Kaplan's discomfort with anthropologists who "search for the authentic self" is ironic, for it is this very search which distinguishes anthropology and illuminates a distinctive feature of the Western tradition. In an article called "Anthropological Traditions: The Participants Observed," Stanley Diamond (1980) says, "We learned what we had always known but somehow never really understood, namely, that anthropology was an aspect of the intellectual history of Western civilization—at its worst the mortician of that civilization—laying out and presenting victimized cultures to public scrutiny, after the explorer, trader, soldier, missionary and administrator had done their work. *But at its most authentic it was the discipline reflecting the self-consciousness of our own society in crisis.*" [emphasis mine]

The "crisis" to which Diamond refers, and the "search for the authentic self" against which Kaplan reacts, are, in fact, long-standing, inherent features of the Western tradition. Anthropology is part and parcel of the cultural structure of the West rather than a counter-movement; it gains its legitimacy, it "makes sense," because of this participation. The fact that Kaplan, Diamond and others have expressed discomfort and alarm, however, is an indication that within the fragmented and beleaguered discipline of today's anthropology, a new self-consciousness is emerging which may signal the appearance of what may be termed authentic anthropology. In contrast with Kaplan's use of the term "authentic," I would argue that authentic anthropology is not "everyman's anthropology" but an anthropology committed to humanity, self-conscious of the very cultural tradition that led to its emergence.

In 1968, Clifford Geertz observed that

> At the moment when [anthropology] seems most deliberately removed from our own lives, it is most immediate, when it seems most insistently to be talking about the distant, the strange, the long ago, or the idiosyncratic, it is in fact talking also about the close, the familiar, the contemporary, and the generic. From one point of view, the whole history of the comparative study of religion...can be looked at as but a circuitous, even devious, approach to a rational analysis of our own situation, an evaluation of our own religious traditions while seeming to evaluate only those of exotic others. (Geertz 1968:2)

Anthropology also reflects and perpetuates the West's conception of racial hierarchies as the "natural state" of humankind. As Collins et al. observed (1981:2),

> ...much of our world is already organized on the basis of biology, or to put it more accurately, a folk biology remarkably similar to some of the assertions of eminent scientists who argue that stratifications and institutional arrangements of contemporary society are merely the working out of a biologically determined plan.

> Recurring cycles of racism and classism in anthropology reflect the influence of culture on the ideas and models proposed by scientists; such ideas pervade both academic and leisure-time activities. The training of students in sciences devoted to the study of man provides a cognitive screen leading ultimately to selective perception and, frequently, to confirmation of presuppositions which are then taught as facts.

Victor Turner has, in several books, noted the need to study the cultural structure of the Western tradition, as well as that of other traditions, through the analysis of symbols. This, in his view, is crucial for the emergence of an authentic anthropology.

> I regard mankind as one in essence though manifold in expression, creative and not merely adaptive in his manifoldness. Any serious study of man must follow him wherever he goes and take into serious account what Florian Znaniecki called the "humanistic coefficient," whereby sociocultural systems depend not only for their meaning but also for their existence upon the participation of *conscious* human agents and upon men's relations with one another. It is this factor of "consciousness" which should lead anthropologists into extended study of complex literate cultures where the most articulate conscious voices of values are the "liminoid" poets, philosophers, dramatists, novelists, painters, and the like....

> I would plead with my colleagues to acquire the humanistic skills that would enable them to live more comfortably in those territories where

the masters of human thought and art have long been dwelling. This must be done if a unified science of man, an authentic anthropology, is ever to become possible. (Turner 1974:17-18)

I have suggested that anthropologists should learn, as an essential part of their training, the cultural structure of their own tradition which promotes the need to incorporate the other. Anthropologists must investigate the use of the human other, must seek to understand what kinds of needs are met by the human other. An authentic anthropology thus construed would promote both scientific and humanistic scholarship.

In his book *The Mismeasure of Man,* Stephen Jay Gould (1981:21) points out that "science must be understood as a social phenomenon, a gutsy, human enterprise, not the work of robots, programmed to collect pure information."

> Science, since people must do it, is a socially embedded activity. It progresses by hunch, vision, and intuition. Much of its change through time does not record a closer approach to absolute truth, but the alteration of cultural contexts that influence it so strongly. Facts are not pure and unsullied bits of information; culture also influences what we see and how we see it. Theories, moreover, are not inexorable inductions from facts. The most creative theories are often imaginative visions imposed upon facts; the source of imagination is also strongly cultural.

As humanists, anthropologists must strive to examine the implications of scientific models.

Ernest Becker (1971) argues that the vision of anthropology, as it was seen by the Enlightenment thinkers who sought to comprehend the meaning of all human knowledge, was lost in the following century. Becker sees in American cultural anthropology the rediscovery of the "authentic tradition of the science of man."

> ...an authentic tradition for the science of man...is one that stresses the synthesis of the disciplines in order to focus on the social moral problem....It has to answer the central problem of the science of man..."How to explain human differences?" But in order to make this central problem a meaningful one morally the further question must be asked: "*What* human differences?" And what makes this question so difficult and crucial is that the answer to it must at the same time be a key to the basis for a new moral code. It could not be, as we saw, the difference in hair texture between races, as the early nineteenth century wanted....What, then, is relevant, supremely relevant? Nothing else but the question: "What are the differences *in human freedom,* in societies, across the span of history?" It is only when we ask this question that we can see the moral usefulness of the science of man. (Becker 1971:120-121)

John Messenger (1981), in his short essay called "Socioanthropology: a New Discipline?" argues that "Since increased specialization has all but shattered the traditional holism of anthropology, why not let physical anthropology join biology, archeology join history, anthropological linguistics join linguistics, and cultural anthropology join sociology?''

From the beginning of the 1960's, Dell Hymes has voiced concern about the negative consequences of academic specialization. According to Hymes (1969), the unique historical factors which facilitated the emergence of departmental dominance as the guardian of anthropological knowledge do not exist today. Historically, the unifying factor of departmental anthropology in America was the study of Indian and other ''primitive'' cultures; and departmental anthropology gained prominence with the expansion of universities that followed World War II. The unifying factor does not exist today, but the departmental domain continues as the dominant institutional context of anthropology, and departmental orientations often nullify and distort the real scope and meaning of anthropology. Internally fragmented and compartmentalized, such orientations prevent the emergence of students who are committed to the holistic study of mankind through a ''passionate rationalism'' and a ''tragic humanism.'' The ideology of departmental anthropology rejects the validity of anthropological humanism, and renders the study of anthropology removed from the human context. Hymes advocates the use of anthropology beyond the institutional context of academic departments. He says that ''If the model of academic anthropology remains unchallenged, then not only will anthropology not be reinvented, it will disappear.''

Anthropology has not disappeared, and I do not think that it is possible for it to disappear. As the French anthropologist Claude Levi-Strauss observed (1966), if anthropology dies it will be reborn with some other label. Anthropology meets a need in the Western tradition. Anthropologists, in their eagerness to present anthropology as a science, as a universalistic orientation, have neglected to examine the close relationship between anthropology and the Western tradition, in particular the features of the Judeo-Christian orientation to which I have called attention in this book.

In Chapters One, Five and Six I have argued that the search for the ''authentic self'' (as Kaplan uses the term) is derived from the cultural structure of the West, as established by the Judeo-Christian orientation. In the Judeo-Christian orientation the self is dichotomized into a divinely sanctioned true self and a divinely rejected untrue self. Excluded from the culturally formulated conception of the true self are all the negative, dark sides of human possibility. The Judeo-Christian orientation rejects the enactment of the complexity of the human condition in its representation of divinity. Anthropology seeks to synthesize the true self and the untrue self, inventing and creating the human other who enacts the human possibilities of the self that are excluded in the Western tradition. I suggest that anthropology is a Western cultural phenomenon generated by the Judeo-Christian cultural structure. Modern anthropology was born out of the need in the West to reconcile the true self and the untrue self in comprehending the unity of the self.

Anthropology, as I have pointed out, is not a device for maintaining ethnic boundaries. People everywhere make the distinction between us and the other. *In the anthropological tradition, the other is in us.*

Nor is anthropology to be defined in terms of its focus on the concept of culture. Most anthropologists agree that the investigation of the nature of culture is an area of knowledge within the disciplinary domain of anthropology, more specifically within cultural anthropology, or ethnology. But if anthropology were defined as the study of culture alone, a more appropriate disciplinary label would be "the comparative study of culture," "comparative sociology," or "culturology." Such studies are not confined to any one discipline, nor do they distinguish any particular intellectual tradition. The study of culture has been done in many different intellectual traditions; to trace its history, one would have to describe the sociological and historical analyses done by Chinese, Islamic, Indian and other traditions. Many different factors promote what I would call "culture consciousness," which is related to a self-conscious maintenance of ethnic identity as well as philosophical speculations concerning reality.

"Culture consciousness" is promoted by many factors. (1) When a group invades and establishes political control over other groups, people become self-conscious of their ethnic identity; the subordinated groups frequently emulate the customs of the dominant groups while at the same time striving to maintain the distinctiveness of their way of life. (2) Many ancient emperors such as Darius of Persia and Ashoka of India tolerated, and in many ways actually promoted, cultural pluralism within their empires, which incorporated several culturally diverse groups. (3) Certain types of social stratification such as the caste system promote the self-conscious creation of differences in group customs among peoples bound together politically and economically. (4) Philosophical traditions that encourage skepticism and speculation about what is customarily held to be true, such as the sophist tradition of ancient Greece, have often made discourse on relativism of knowledge and morality an essential part of education.

Anthropology's focus on the analysis of culture is recent, having occurred only during the past hundred years; this focus is not what distinguishes anthropology. Nor does the methodology of participant observation distinguish anthropology from other disciplines. As I have argued in Chapters One, Five and Six, modern anthropology is rooted in the Judeo-Christian orientation of dichotomizing the self, incorporating the human other to integrate the self, and not in the philosophical, sociological or historical discourses on the nature of humankind or cultural differences that occur in all intellectual traditions. Anthropology is not an extension of ethnicity nor is it a demystifier of ethnicity. *Anthropology brings the human*

*other into us, i.e., the West, and provides various models of dichotomy and
unity of humankind.*

An authentic anthropology must study the mythology of the human other
of the Western tradition. It is in this cultural structure that anthropology
defines itself. As Murray Leaf notes (1979:12): "Far from being unable to
escape the bonds of our culture, we may be at the point of obtaining, as a
trans-cultural experimental discipline, a new level of the special freedom
that consists in understanding human understanding itself."

The study of the history of anthropology presents an opportunity and an
avenue through which an authentic anthropology may be forged. In becoming authentic anthropologists, students must understand how anthropology
fits in the Western tradition; they must learn to identify the cultural structure which promotes anthropological inquiry, becoming sensitive to cultural
biases. The study of the history of anthropology can serve as an instrument
to investigate the relevance and consequences of current anthropological
research, relating the present to the past and helping establish guidelines. It
can bring the various sub-disciplines together, promote a dialogue among
the various specialists and promote unification of schismogenic
departments in the name of a common goal of representing humanity
humanistically. The human sciences tend to be unclear of focus, are bombarded with conflicting interests, and are for the most part unable to
address the major questions of human survival. Anthropologists, rather
than contributing to this trend, should strive to analyze their history and
cultural structure. By becoming self-conscious of the strengths and pitfalls
of the Western tradition they have a greater chance to act in ways that even
if they are not free of cultural bias, which is humanly impossible, at least
reflect the greater wisdom born of historical consciousness.

Bibliography

Anderson, R.T.
1967   "The Flirtation of Anthropology and History," Research Studies 35.
Arens, W.
1979   The Man-Eating Myth: Anthropology and Anthropophagy. New York: Oxford University Press.
Barth, F.
1969   Ethnic Groups and Boundaries: The Social Organization of Cultural Differences. Boston: Little, Brown and Co.
Baudet, H.
1965   Paradise on Earth: Thoughts on European Images of Non-European Man. New Haven: Yale University Press.
Beals, R.
1953   "Acculturation," in A.L. Kroeber, ed. Anthropology Today. Chicago: University of Chicago Press.
Becker, E.
1971   The Lost Science of Man. New York: George Braziller.
Benedict, R.
1948   "Anthropology and the Humanities," American Anthropologist 51.
Bernheimer, R.
1952   Wild Men in the Middle Ages: A Study in Art, Sentiment, and Demonology. Cambridge: Harvard University Press.
Berkhofer, R.F., Jr.
1978   The White Man's Indian: Images of the American Indian from Columbus to the Present. New York: Random House.
Bohannon, P., and M. Glazer, eds.
1973   High Points in Anthropology. New York: A.A. Knopf.
Brandt, A.M.
1978   "Racism and Research: The Case of the Tuskegee Syphilis Study," Hastings Center Magazine.
Brew, J.O.
1968   One Hundred Years of Anthropology. New York: Oxford University Press.
Bucher, B.
1981   Icon and Conquest: A Structural Analysis of the Illustrations of de Bry's Great Voyages. Chicago: University of Chicago Press.

Burrow, J.W.
1966   Evolution and Society: A Study in Victorian Social Theory. London: Cambridge University Press.

Carr, E.H.
1961   What is History? New York: Vintage Books.

Chiapelli, F., ed.
1976   First Images of America: The Impact of the New World on the Old. Berkeley: University of California Press.

Cohen, A.
1976   Two-Dimensional Man: An Essay on the Anthropology of Power and Symbolism in Complex Society. Berkeley: University of California Press.

Cohn, B.S.
1980   "History and Anthropology: The State of Play," Comparative Studies in Society and History 22 (2).

Collingwood, R.G.
1946   The Idea of History. London: Oxford University Press.

Collins, M.S., I.W. Wainer and T.A. Bremner, eds.
1981   Science and the Question of Human Equality. Boulder, Colorado: Westview Press, 1981.

Curtin, P.D.
1964   The Image of Africa: British Ideas and Action, 1780-1850. Madison: The University of Wisconsin Press.

Darnell, R.
1974   Readings in the History of Anthropology. New York: Harper and Row.

Dawson, R.
1967   The Chinese Chameleon: An Analysis of European Conceptions of Chinese Civilization. London: Oxford University Press.

de Mille, R.
1980   The Don Juan Papers: Further Castaneda Controversies. California: Ross-Erikson Publishers.

De Vos, G.
1975   "Ethnic Pluralism: Conflict and Accommodation," in G. De Vos and L. Romanucci-Ross, eds. Ethnic Identity. Palo Alto: Mayfield Publishing Co.

Diamond, S.
1980   Anthropology: Ancestors and Heirs. The Hague: Mouton Publishers.

Dolgin, J.L., D.S. Kemnitzer, and D.M. Schneider, eds.
1977   Symbolic Anthropology: A Reader in the Study of Symbols and Meanings. New York: Columbia University Press.

Dudley, E., and M.E. Novak, eds.
1972   The Wild Man Within: An Image in Western Thought from the Renaissance to Romanticism. Pittsburgh, Pennsylvania: University of Pittsburgh Press.

Eco, U.
1979   A Theory of Semiotics. Bloomington: Indiana University Press.

Elias, N.
1978   The Civilizing Process: The Development of Manners. New York: Urizen Books.

Evans-Pritchard, E.E.
1961   Anthropology and History. Manchester: Manchester University Press.
Fabian, J.
1983   Time and the Other: How Anthropology Makes its Object. New York:
            Columbia University Press.
Fenton, W.N.
1979   "J.F. Lafitau (1681-1746), Precursor of Scientific Anthropology,"
            Southwestern Journal of Anthropology 25.
Finley, I.M.
1965   "Myth, Memory, and History," History and Theory 5 (3).
Firth, R.
1973   Symbols: Public and Private. Ithaca, New York: Cornell University
            Press.
Freeman, D.
1983   Margaret Mead and Samoa: The Making and Unmaking of an Anthro-
            pological Myth. Cambridge, Mass.: Harvard University Press.
Friedman, J.B.
1981   The Monstrous Races in Medieval Art and Thought. Cambridge, Mass.:
            Harvard University Press.
Geertz, C.
1968   Islam Observed. Chicago: University of Chicago Press.
1971   Myth, Symbol, and Culture. New York: W.W. Norton and Co., Inc.
1973   The Interpretation of Cultures. New York: Basic Books, Inc.,
            Publishers.
Gilman, S.C.
1982   "Degeneracy and Race in the Nineteenth Century: The Impact of
            Clinical Medicine," The Journal of Ethnic Studies 10 (4).
Gould, S.J.
1981   The Mismeasure of Man. New York: W.W. Norton and Co.
Greene, J.
1981   Science, Ideology, and World View: Essays in the History of Evolu-
            tionary Ideas. Berkeley: University of California Press.
Gruber, J.
1973   "Forerunners," in R. Naroll and F. Naroll, eds. Main Currents in
            Cultural Anthropology. New York: Appleton-Century-Crofts.
1974   "Brixham Cave and the Antiquity of Man," in R. Darnell, ed. Readings
            in the History of Anthropology. New York: Harper and Row.
Gupta, J.D.
1975   "Ethnicity, Language Demands and National Development in India,"
            in N. Glazer and D.P. Moynihan, eds. Ethnicity. Cambridge, Mass.:
            Harvard University Press.
Haddon, C.
1934   History of Anthropology. London: Watts and Co.
Haller, J.S., Jr.
1970   "The Species Problem: Nineteenth Century Concepts of Racial Infer-
            iority in the Origin of Man Controversy," American Anthropologist 72.
Hallowell, A.I.
1965   "The History of Anthropology as an Anthropological Problem,"
            Journal of the History of the Behavioral Sciences 1.

Hanke, L.
  1959   Aristotle and the American Indians: A Study in Race Prejudice in the
            Modern World. Bloomington: Indiana University Press.
Harris, M.
  1968   The Rise of Anthropological Theory: A History of Theories of Culture.
            New York: Thomas Y. Crowell Co.
  1979   Cultural Materialism: The Struggle for a Science of Culture. New York:
            Vintage Books.
Hatch, E.
  1973   Theories of Man and Culture. New York: Columbia University Press.
  1983   Culture and Morality. New York: Columbia University Press.
Hays, H.R.
  1958   From Ape to Angel: An Informal History of Social Anthropology.
            New York: Alfred A. Knopf.
Heine-Geldern, R.
  1964   "One Hundred Years of Ethnological Theory in the German-Speaking
            Countries," Current Anthropology 51.
Herder, J.G.
  1885   Ideas of the Philosophy of the History of Mankind. London: Luke
            Hansard.
Hinsley, C.M., Jr.
  1981   Savages and Scientists: The Smithsonian Institution and the Develop-
            ment of American Anthropology, 1846-1910. Washington, D.C.:
            Smithsonian Institution Press.
Hodgen, M.T.
  1964   Early Anthropology in the Sixteenth and Seventeenth Centuries.
            Philadelphia: University of Pennsylvania Press.
Honigmann, J.J.
  1967   The Development of Anthropological Ideas. Homewood, Ill.: The
            Dorsey Press.
Honour, H.
  1977   The New Golden Land: European Images of America from the Dis-
            coveries to the Present Time. New York: Random House.
Hsu, F.L. K.
  1973   "Prejudice and its Intellectual Effect in American Anthropology,"
            American Anthropologist 75.
Hudson, C.
  1973   "The Historical Approach in Anthropology," in J.J. Honigmann, ed.
            Handbook of Social and Cultural Anthropology. Chicago: Rand
            McNally and Co.
Hughes, E.C.
  1974   "Who Studies Whom?" Human Organization 33.
Hughes, H.S.
  1964   History as Art and as Science: Twin Vistas on the Past. New York:
            Harper and Row.
Hume, D.
  1954   "Of National Character," in The Philosophical Works of David Hume.
            Boston: Little, Brown.

Hymes, D.
1962   "On Studying the History of Anthropology," Kroeber Anthropological Society 26.
1969   Reinventing Anthropology. New York: Random House.
Jennings, S.F.
1975   The Invasion of America: Indians, Colonialism, and the Cant of Conquest. New York: W.W. Norton.
Jones, J.
1981   Bad Blood. New York: Free Press.
Kaplan, D.
1974   "The Anthropology of Authenticity: Everyman his own Anthropologist," American Anthropologist 76.
Kardiner, A., and E. Preble
1963   They Studied Man. New York: New American Library.
Kennedy, J.H.
1950   Jesuit and Savage in New France. New Haven: Yale Historical Publications.
Kennedy, K.A.R.
1974   "Race and Culture," in R. Naroll and F. Naroll, eds. Main Currents in Cultural Anthropology. New York: Appleton-Century Crofts.
Kroeber, A.L.
1917   "The Superorganic," American Anthropologist 19.
1935   "History and Science in Anthropology," American Anthropologist 37.
_____ and C. Kluckhohn
1952   Culture: A Critical Review of Concepts and Definitions. New York: Vintage Books.
Kuhn, T.
1962   The Structure of Scientific Revolutions. Chicago: University of Chicago Press.
Leach, E.R.
1972   "Pulleyar and the Lord Buddha: An Aspect of Religious Syncretism in Ceylon," in W.A. Lessa and E.Z. Vogt, eds. Reader in Comparative Religion (3rd ed.) New York: Harper and Row.
Leaf, M.J.
1979   Man, Mind, and Science: A History of Anthropology. New York: Columbia University Press.
Levi-Strauss, C.
1963   Structural Anthropology. New York: Basic Books.
1966   "Anthropology: Its Achievements and its Future," Current Anthropology 7.
Lewis, I.
1977   "Introduction" in I. Lewis, ed. Symbols and Sentiments: Cross-Cultural Studies in Symbolism. New York: Academic Press.
Linton, R.
1937   "One Hundred Per-Cent American," The American Mercury 40.
Long, C.H.
1978a   "Human Centers: An Essay on Method in the History of Religion," Soundings LXI.
1978b   Primitive/Civilized: The Locus of a Problem. History of Religions 20.

Long, E.
1970   History of Jamaica, Vol. II, Book III. London: Frank Cass and Co.
Lovejoy, A.O., et al.
1935   A Documentary History of Primitivism and Related Ideas. Baltimore, Md.: Johns Hopkins Press.
Lowie, R.H.
1938   The History of Ethnological Theory. New York: Holt, Rinehart and Winston.
1953   "Ethnography, Cultural and Social Anthropology," American Anthropologist 55.
Malefijt, A.D.
1976   Images of Man: A History of Anthropological Thought. New York: A.A. Knopf.
Mandelbaum, D.G., G.W. Lasker, and E.M. Albert, eds.
1967   The Teaching of Anthropology. Berkeley: University of California Press.
Mead, G.H.
1934   Mind, Self and Society. Chicago: University of Chicago Press.
Mead, M.
1949   Coming of Age in Samoa. New York: New American Library.
1963   Sex and Temperament in Three Primitive Societies. New York: New American Library.
Messenger, J.C.
1981   "Socioanthropology: A New Discipline," Anthropology Newsletter 7.
Montagu, A.
1965   The Idea of Race. Lincoln: University of Nebraska Press.
Montaigne, M.
1958   Essays. New York: Penguin Books.
Nash, G.B.
1974   Red, White and Black: The Peoples of Early America. Englewood Cliffs, N.J.: Prentice-Hall.
Needham, R.J.
1959   Science and Civilization in China. Cambridge: Cambridge University Press.
1980   Lecture, Department of Religion, University of North Carolina, Chapel Hill.
O'Flaherty, W.D.
1973   Siva: The Erotic Ascetic. New York: Oxford University Press.
Ortner, S.
1973   "On Key Symbols," American Anthropologist 75.
Pagels, E.
1981   The Gnostic Gospels. New York: Vintage Books.
Pandian, J.
1974   "Factors in Fieldwork," Newsletter of the American Anthropological Association 15.
1975a   "Participant Observation, Liminality, and the Science of Man," The International Journal of Contemporary Sociology 2.
1975b   "Anthropological Fieldwork, Empathy and the Crisis of the Apocalyptic Man," Man in India 55.

| 1977 | "The Goddess of Chastity and the Politics of Ethnicity in the Tamil Society of South Asia," Contributions to Asian Studies 10. |

1977   "The Goddess of Chastity and the Politics of Ethnicity in the Tamil Society of South Asia," Contributions to Asian Studies 10.

1978   "The Hindu Caste System and Muslim Ethnicity," Ethnohistory 25.

1981   "The Goddess Kannagi," in J. Preston, ed. Mother Worship. Chapel Hill: University of North Carolina Press.

1982   "The Teaching of the History of Anthropology as a Course on Western Intellectual Tradition," Newsletter of the American Anthropological Association 20.

1983a   "The Sacred Symbol of the Mother Goddess in a Tamil Village," in G.R. Gupta, ed. Religion in Modern India. New Delhi: Vikas Publications.

1983b   "Political Emblems of Caste Identity," Anthropological Quarterly 56.

1984a   "The Anthropological Quest for a Sanskritic Civilization of India," in M.D. Zamora, ed. Social Change in Modern South Asia. Ranchi: Anthropological Studies.

1984b   "Essay on the State of Anthropology: Anthropology in the Humanities," Newsletter of the American Anthropological Association 25.

In Press "The Mythology of the Other and the Roots of Modern Anthropology," The International Journal of Contemporary Anthropology.

Pelto, P.J., and G.H. Pelto
1978   Anthropological Research. Cambridge: Cambridge University Press.

Poliakov, L.
1971   The Aryan Myth: A History of Racist and Nationalist Ideas in Europe. New York: Basic Books.

Radcliffe-Brown, A.R.
1952   "Historical Note on British Social Anthropology," American Anthropologist 54.

Rowe, J.H.
1965   "The Renaissance Foundations of Anthropology," American Anthropologist 67.

Sahlins, M.
1983   "Other Times, Other Customs: The Anthropology of History," American Anthropologist 85 (3).

Sapir, E.
1917   "Do We Need a Superorganic," American Anthropologist 19.

Silverman, S., ed.
1981   Totems and Teachers: Perspectives on the History of Anthropology. New York: Columbia University Press.

Slotkin, J.S.
1965   Readings in Early Anthropology. Chicago: Aldine Publishing.

Smith, H.
1958   The Religions of Man. New York: Harper and Row.

Smith, S.S.
1810   (1787) An Essay on the Causes of the Variety of Complexion and Figure in the Human Species. New Brunswick.

Spitzka, E.C.
1903   "A Study of the Brain of the Late Major Wesley Powell," American Anthropologist 10/12.

Stanton, W.
   1960   The Leopard's Spots: Scientific Attitudes Toward Race in America,
            1815-1859. Chicago: University of Chicago Press.
Stepan, N.
   1981   The Idea of Race in Science: Great Britain 1800-1960. Hamden: Archon
            Books.
Stocking, G.W., Jr.
   1968   Race, Culture and Evolution: Essays in the History of Anthropology.
            New York: Free Press.
   1974   A Franz Boas Reader: The Shaping of American Anthropology, 1883-
            1911. Chicago: University of Chicago Press.
   1983   Observers Observed: Essays on Ethnographic Fieldwork, Madison:
            University of Wisconsin Press.
Sturtevant, W.C.
   1966   "Anthropology, History, and Ethnohistory," Ethnohistory 13.
Taylor, H.O.
   1925   The Medieval Mind: A History of the Development of Thought and
            Emotion in the Middle Ages (4th ed.) London.
Thoresen, T.H.H., ed.
   1975   Toward a Science of Man: Essays in the History of Anthropology.
            The Hague: Mouton Pub.
Tuchman, B.W.
   1979   A Distant Mirror: The Calamitous 14th Century. New York: Ballantine
            Books.
Turner, V.W.
   1969   The Ritual Process. Chicago: Aldine.
   1974   Dramas, Fields, and Metaphors: Symbolic Action in Human Society.
            Ithaca: Cornell University Press.
Tylor, E.
   1871   Primitive Culture: Researches into the Development of Mythology,
            Philosophy, Religion, Language, Art and Custom. London: J. Murray.
Vansina, J.
   1961   Oral Tradition: A Study in Historical Methodology, Chicago: Aldine
            Publishing Co.
Voget, F.W.
   1975   A History of Ethnology. New York: Holt, Rinehart and Winston.
Wagner, R.
   1975   The Invention of Culture. Englewood Cliffs, N.J.: Prentice-Hall, Inc.
Wallace, A.F.C.
   1956   "Revitalization Movements," American Anthropologist 58.
   1970   Culture and Personality (2nd ed.) New York: Random House.
Ware, C., ed.
   1940   The Cultural Approach to the Study of History. New York: Columbia
            University Press.
White, H.
   1972   "The Forms of Wildness: Archeology of an Idea," in E. Dudley and
            M.E. Novak, eds. The Wild Man Within. Pittsburgh: University of
            Pittsburgh Press.

White, L.
1959   "The Concept of Culture," American Anthropologist 61.
Wolf, E.
1964   Anthropology. Princeton: Princeton University Press.
1982   Europe and the People Without History. Berkeley: University of California Press.